# THE GOODNESS OF GOD

By Dr. Angel A. Abakah

# Dedication

This book is dedicated to:

My mother, Mrs. Dina Arkoful. I am thankful for your prayers, wisdom teachings, and your blessings over my life.

My wife: Lady Dr. Angelina Abakah. I am grateful for your love, support, advice, prayer and encouragement.

My Children: Miracle, Heaven, Holy-Elle, Godbless and Trinity. Thank you for your love and thank you for believing in me. I love you all.

Ghana Wesley UMC, Brooklyn: Thank you for your prayers.

# Preface

Each chapter of this book is crafted to guide readers deeper into the heart of God, offering practical insights, biblical truth, and encouragement for every step of the faith journey. By weaving together Scripture, authentic stories, and reflective questions, the 'Goodness of God' aims to inspire hope and strengthen the reader's relationship with God, equipping believers to see His goodness at work in every circumstance and to live with unwavering trust in His promises; finding hope, faith, and strength in every season.

The Goodness of God is a faith-filled journey through the character of God, not just when life is easy, but even in seasons of pain, delay, and uncertainty. The book invites readers to see God's character through Scripture, personal reflection, and real-life stories, reminding us that His goodness is constant, unconditional, and unfailing.

# Introduction

*The Goodness of God*

There is one truth that has echoed through generations, sustained the weary, restored the broken, and anchored the souls of countless believers: God is good. It is a simple declaration, often spoken, often sung, but not always fully understood. For many, the Goodness of God is easy to proclaim in seasons of abundance, yet difficult to grasp in moments of pain, confusion, and loss. This book is an invitation to journey deeper to move beyond surface-level acknowledgment into a life-transforming revelation of the Goodness of God.

We live in a world filled with contradictions. Joy and sorrow often walk side by side. Faith is sometimes tested by circumstances that seem to challenge what we believe about God's nature. In such moments, questions arise: *If God is good, why do we suffer? If He is loving, why does He allow pain? If He is faithful, why do we feel forgotten?* These questions are not signs of weak faith - they are the cries of a heart longing to understand the character of God more deeply.

The truth is that God's goodness is not dependent on our circumstances. It does not fluctuate with our emotions, nor do our trials diminish it. The goodness of God is constant, unwavering, and eternal. It is woven into the very fabric of who He is. From the beginning of creation to the unfolding of redemption, Scripture reveals a God whose goodness is evident in His works, His words, and His ways.

*Psalm 100:5: For the LORD is good; His mercy is everlasting, and His truth endures to all generations.*

From Genesis to Revelation, from Eden to eternity, the Bible is a love story inspired by a God who is good, does good, and desires good for His people. This book is a journey into that truth - that even when life doesn't feel good, God still is. And because He is good, He will do you good.

The book seeks to uncover that truth, not merely as a theological concept, but as a living reality. The goodness of God is not just something to be studied; it is something to be experienced. It is seen in His provision, felt in His presence, and revealed in God's promises. Even in the darkest valleys, His goodness remains a guiding light, leading us forward with hope and assurance.

Throughout these pages, we will explore the many dimensions of God's goodness. We will see it in creation, where every detail reflects His intentional care. We will encounter it in His mercy, which meets us in our failures and restores us with grace. We will recognize it in His faithfulness, which endures even when we fall short. And ultimately, we will behold it most clearly in the person and work of Jesus Christ, the ultimate expression of God's goodness toward humanity.

Yet this journey is not only about understanding God, but also about transformation. When we truly grasp the goodness of God, it changes how we see everything. It reshapes our perspective on suffering, strengthens our trust in uncertainty, and deepens our relationship with Him. It teaches us to worship not just for what God does, but for who He is. It empowers us to reflect His goodness in our own lives, becoming vessels of His love, kindness, and compassion to a world in need.

There is a profound difference between knowing about God's goodness and truly believing in it. Knowledge informs the mind, but revelation transforms the heart. This book is written with the prayer that as you read, the Holy Spirit will illuminate the truth of God's goodness in a personal and powerful way. That which begins as words on a page will become a living testimony within your soul.

Perhaps you come to this book with a heart full of gratitude, already convinced of God's goodness through personal experience. Or perhaps you come with questions, doubts, or even pain that has made it difficult to trust in His goodness. Wherever you find yourself, you are welcome here. This journey is for anyone who desires to know God more deeply and to experience the fullness of His nature and goodness.

God's goodness is not reserved for a select few; it is available to all who seek Him. It is not something we earn, but something we receive. It is not distant or unreachable, but near and ever-present. Even now, His goodness surrounds you, sustains you, and calls you into a deeper relationship with Him.

As you turn these pages, may the Holy Spirit open your eyes to see the goodness of God in ways you have never seen before. May your heart be strengthened to trust Him in every season. And may your life become a testimony of His goodness; One that shines brightly for others to see.

For in the end, the goodness of God is not just a message to be shared, but also a reality to be lived.

# Table of Contents

# Chapter 1: God Is Good, All the Time

The phrase "God is good, all the time" has echoed through religious institutions, especially churches for generations. It's more than a slogan; it is a declaration of faith. How we see or perceive God can make God become that reality for us. God is good in big things as well as in little things.

In my personal life, how I experienced God's goodness was not always in big, dramatic, and spectacular moments, but often in the quiet, unexpected ways. It was in the strength I found when I thought I had none left. It was in the doors that opened just when others closed. Sometimes the peace that came over me in the middle of confusion.

There were times I didn't understand what God was doing, yet looking back, I can see God's hand guiding me, protecting me, and providing for me. What felt like delays were divine timing. *You can think about your own story.*

These are testimonies I cannot deny. He made a way where there was no way. When I was weak, God became my strength. When I was lost, God directed my path. When I felt forgotten, God reminded me that I was never alone.

God's goodness chased me when I didn't realize it, and His mercy covered me when I didn't deserve it. Even in my life before knowing Christ, I still experienced glimpses of God's goodness, but I just could not attribute those happenings as the acts of God in my life.

In my struggles, He reminded me to trust Him. In my waiting, He taught me patience using the people around me. In the stillness, He would often speak peace to my heart.

Friends, I cannot say every day will be good, but I do believe that every day, God will be good. His grace will carry you, His love will sustain you, and His faithfulness will never fail you

The goodness of God is not just what He does, but who He is. Psalm 100:5 says, *"For the Lord is good and His love endures forever."* The word "good" in Hebrew - tov - means pleasant, joyful, excellent, and beneficial. From the first chapter of Genesis, everything God made was good. Creation itself was the overflow of His goodness. God never made anything to be bad. Everything was made to be good and produce goodness.

Even when Adam and Eve fell, God's goodness was not withdrawn. It was revealed through mercy. He clothed them, protected them, and began a plan for redemption that would culminate in Jesus Christ, the ultimate expression of divine goodness.

To say "God is good" is to affirm that His character never changes, even when our circumstances do. God's character is one of the most comforting and stabilizing truths in the life of a believer. While everything around us can shift, our health, relationships, finances, emotions, and circumstances, God remains the same. He is not influenced by time, pressure, or uncertainty. His nature is constant, dependable, and unchanging. This truth becomes an anchor for the soul, especially during seasons of instability.

The Bible clearly affirms this: *"For I am the Lord, I change not"* (Malachi 3:6). This means that God's love does not weaken when life gets difficult. His faithfulness does not fade when we feel discouraged. His promises do not expire when circumstances seem to contradict them. What God has been, He still is - and what He has promised, He will still perform. Hallelujah!

Human life is marked by change. One day things may seem to be going well, and the next day everything can feel uncertain. People can change, feelings can fluctuate, and situations can shift without warning. But God does not move with the tides of life. He is steady. He is sure. He is reliable. When everything else feels unstable, God remains a firm foundation.

This unchanging nature of God is especially important when we face trials. In difficult moments, it can feel as though God has changed or moved away from us. But the truth is, it is not God who moves; it is often our perspective that becomes clouded by pain or fear. God is still good, even when life is hard. He is still present, even when He feels distant from us. He is still working, even when we cannot see immediate results.

Hebrews 13:8 says, *"Jesus Christ the same yesterday, and today, and forever."* This reminds us that the same Jesus who healed the sick, provided for the needy, and calmed storms is still active today. His power has not diminished. His compassion has not weakened. His authority has not changed. The same grace available in the past is available today.

God's unchanging character also means that His love is consistent. Unlike human love, which can sometimes be conditional or influenced by emotions, God's love is steady and unconditional. Romans 8:38-39 reminds us that nothing can separate us from the love of God. Not hardship, not failure, not uncertainty, nothing.

When circumstances change, we are often tempted to base our faith on what we see or feel. But true faith is rooted in who God is, not in what is happening around us. If we only trust God when life is good, our faith will be unstable. But when we learn to trust in His unchanging nature, our faith becomes strong and resilient.

God's promises are also tied to His unchanging character. If God could change, then His promises would not be secure. But because He remains the same, we can trust every word He has spoken. What He has said about provision, protection, peace, and purpose still stands, regardless of our current circumstances.

In practical terms, this truth invites us to shift our focus. Instead of being overwhelmed by changing situations, we fix our eyes on the unchanging God. We remind ourselves daily of His faithfulness and declare His promises. We choose to trust His character even when we do not understand His timing because we are convinced that God is good.

Ultimately, God's goodness gives us hope. It means that no matter how uncertain life becomes, we are not at the mercy of chaos. We are held by a God who is constant, faithful, and true. His character is our refuge. His consistency is our peace.

So, when circumstances change, and they will, remember this: God has not changed. He is still good. He is still faithful. He is still in control. And He is still working all things together for good.

Another powerful dimension of God's goodness is seen in His purposes and plans. Even when our circumstances shift unexpectedly, God's ultimate plan for our lives remains intact. What may feel like a disruption to us is never confusing to God. He is not reacting to events as they happen; He is sovereign over them. Isaiah 46:10 declares that He "declares the end from the beginning." This means that before we ever encounter a change, God has already seen it, allowed it, and prepared a way through it.

Sometimes we interpret changes in our lives as setbacks, delays, or even signs that God has forgotten us. But God's unchanging character assures us that He is always intentional. He does not abandon His work halfway. Philippians 1:6 reminds us that *"He who has begun a good work in you will perform it until the day of Jesus Christ."* Even when our path looks different from what we expected, God's commitment to His purpose in our lives never changes. God is good!

This truth is especially important when we face seasons of waiting. Waiting can feel like nothing is happening, like God is silent or inactive. But God's character tells us otherwise. He is always working behind the scenes. Just because we cannot see movement does not mean there is no progress. God's timing is not rushed, delayed, or accidental; it is perfect. His consistency ensures that every promise unfolds at the right time.

Additionally, God's unchanging character means that His standards of righteousness do not shift with culture or time. In a world where values are constantly evolving, God remains the same in His holiness, truth, and justice. What He calls right is always right, and what He calls wrong is always wrong. This gives believers a firm moral foundation in a world of uncertainty. We are not left to guess what truth is - God's character defines it.

At the same time, His unchanging holiness is perfectly balanced with His unchanging mercy. God does not lower His standards, but He also never withholds His grace from those who come to Him. Lamentations 3:22-23 says, *"It is of the Lord's mercies that we are not consumed, because his compassions fail not. They are new every morning."* Notice this: even though God never changes, His mercy meets us fresh every day. His consistency does not make Him distant; it rather makes Him dependable.

When we truly understand that God's character never changes, it transforms how we respond to life. Instead of panic, we develop peace. Instead of fear, we grow in trust. Instead of being controlled by circumstances, we become grounded in truth. We begin to live with confidence, knowing that the same God who was faithful yesterday will be faithful today and forever.

This also gives us the strength to endure. Trials may come, but they do not have the final word. Emotions may fluctuate, but they do not define our reality. Circumstances may shift, but they do not change who God is. When everything around us feels uncertain, we hold onto the certainty of God's nature.

In the end, the goodness of God is not just a theological idea; it is a daily source of strength. It is what allows us to keep moving forward when life feels unstable. It is what gives us the courage to trust when we do not understand. And it is what anchors our faith in every season.

So, no matter what changes you may face, stand firm in this truth: God's goodness is sure. His plans are sure. His mercy is unfailing. His truth is unshakable. And because He never changes, we can trust Him completely, all the time.

# Chapter 2: The True Nature and Character of God

**The Foundation of Faith.**

Every relationship depends on trust, and every trust depends on knowing someone's character. You can't trust what you don't know - and that's why many people struggle to trust God. They know about Him, but they don't truly know His nature.

The strength of your faith will always match the depth of your understanding of God's Character.

*Hebrews 11:6 says,*

*"But without faith it is impossible to please Him, for he who comes to God must believe that He is, and that He is a rewarder of those who diligently seek Him."*

If you believe God is unpredictable or harsh, you'll serve Him with fear. But if you believe He is loving and good, you'll walk with confidence and peace. To understand God's goodness, we must understand who He is at His core.

**God Is Good by Nature, Not by Choice**

We sometimes say, *"God chooses to be good."*

But the truth is deeper: God is not good because He chooses to be - He is good because He cannot be otherwise. Malachi 3:6 says, *"For I am the LORD, I do not change; Therefore, you are not consumed, O sons of Jacob."*

Goodness is not an action God performs; it's His essence.

When Moses asked to see God's glory, the Lord responded in Exodus 33:19:

*"I will cause all My goodness to pass before you, and I will proclaim My name, the Lord, in your presence."*

Notice what God called His glory - His goodness!

His nature, His name, His power, and His glory are all expressions of one reality: God is good.

*You and I can have good moments, but God is goodness itself. He is not merely loving - He is love.* (1 John 4:8)

He is not merely righteous, He is righteousness.

He is not merely truthful, He is truth.

Everything that is truly good in this universe originates in Him.

The Goodness of God is unchanging.

The world changes every day, people change, systems shift, governments rise and fall, but God's nature never changes.

Malachi 3:6 says,

*"I, the Lord, do not change."*

And James 1:17 declares,

*"Every good and perfect gift is from above, coming down from the Father of lights, who does not change like shifting shadows."*

Think about that: there are no shadows in God's character.

He's not kind one day and distant the next. He doesn't wake up moody. His goodness does not depend on your behavior or your circumstances. He is as good today as He was when He created the world, as He was when Jesus walked the earth, and as He will be when time itself ends.

Your situation may change, but His nature never will. Let us see how His goodness is revealed in His names.

**God's Goodness Revealed in His Names**

Throughout Scripture, God revealed Himself through His names, each one showing an aspect of His character and goodness:

- *Jehovah Jireh* - The Lord will provide (Genesis 22:14). His goodness meets your needs.
- *Jehovah Rapha* - The Lord who heals you (Exodus 15:26). His goodness restores what is broken.

- *Jehovah Shalom* - The Lord is peace (Judges 6:24). His goodness calms your storms.
- *Jehovah Raah* - The Lord my Shepherd (Psalm 23:1). His goodness guides and protects you.
- *Jehovah Tsidkenu* - The Lord our righteousness (Jeremiah 23:6). His goodness covers your sin.

Each name is a doorway into understanding how deeply good God truly is. His goodness is not abstract; it's personal, practical, and present.

**The Goodness of God Is Seen in His Patience**

If God were only holy but not good, none of us would survive a single day. But His holiness is wrapped in mercy, and His justice is balanced with compassion.

Psalm 145:8-9 says:

*"The Lord is gracious and compassionate, slow to anger and rich in love. The Lord is good to all; He has compassion on all He has made."*

Think about that, good to all. Not just to the perfect, the powerful, or the prayerful, but to all. Even those who reject Him still breathe His air and live under His mercy. That's goodness beyond comprehension.

If God were quick to anger and slow to forgive, none of us would stand. But His patience proves His love. His kindness is not weakness - it's the evidence of His goodness.

**God's Goodness and His Justice**

Some people struggle to reconcile God's goodness with His justice. "How can a good God allow judgment?" They ask. But God's justice is part of His goodness.

Imagine a world where evil goes unpunished, where injustice never meets accountability. That wouldn't be goodness - that would be chaos.

Because God is good, He must confront evil. Because He loves righteousness, He must oppose wickedness. Even His judgments flow from His goodness - they are the surgeon's knife that cuts, in order to heal.

At the cross, we see the perfect union of justice and mercy.

Sin was judged, and sinners were forgiven - both acts of divine goodness. Now let's see God's goodness in our Lord Jesus Christ.

**God's Goodness in Jesus Christ**

Jesus is the visible image of the invisible God. Colossians 1:15 says, *"He is the image of the invisible God, the firstborn over all creation."*

If you want to know what God is like, look at Jesus. Every word He spoke, every person He touched, every miracle He performed was a window into the Father's heart.

*Jesus was good to me. (I was saved by grace through faith in Christ Jesus)*

*He was good to the sinner. (John 8:10-11, Luke 19:10)*

*He was good to the sick. (Matthew 14:14, Mark 1:40-42)*

*He was good to the rejected. (Mark 5:25-34)*

*He was good to little children. (Matthew 19:13-15)*

*He was good even to those who crucified Him. (Luke 23:24)*

*That is, God is good to all. Psalm 145:9 - The LORD is good to all, and His tender mercies are over all His works.*

When we look at Jesus, we see that God's goodness is not just theoretical - it is practical and incarnational because it takes on flesh and walks among us. *"How God anointed Jesus of Nazareth with the Holy Spirit and power, and how He went around doing good and healing all who were under the power of the devil, because God was with Him."* Acts 10:38.

Jesus didn't just preach about goodness - He demonstrated it, and he lived it.

**The Mystery of God's Goodness in Suffering**

Many people question God's goodness when they face pain.

"If God is good," they ask, "why did He allow this?"

It's an honest question that every believer wrestles with. But even in suffering, God's goodness is not absent; it's often hidden, waiting to be revealed.

### <u>God is Good Even On a Hospital Bed:</u>

A few years ago, my mother battled with a terminal disease that required open-heart surgery. Prior to the diagnosis, the doctors gave up on her. The family was told to humbly take her home and allow her to die peacefully. She was in pain yet trusting the healing power of God. The doctors came up with another plan, but that would be a fifty percent chance of surviving or dying. The family prayed for her and trusted in God's direction in the situation. After the prayers, we decided to allow her to have the surgery. As a matter of fact, the doctors knew there was no hope in what they were doing, but they had to do it anyway. The surgery went on as scheduled, but to the surprise of the medical team that worked on her and everyone who knew her predicament, she survived and speedily recovered. The doctors and the nurses were amazed by how such a hopeless situation became hopeful. That was the doing of the Lord….and it is marvelous in our eyes. Listen, there is no hopeless situation. Scripture says that *"against hope, Abraham believed in hope."*

There are moments in life when hope appears to vanish, where circumstances speak louder than promises, facts seem stronger than faith, and reality contradicts what we believe God has said. It is in these moments that the phrase "against hope" becomes real.

To be "against hope" means that everything visible, logical, and natural says, "There is no way forward." It is the place where our expectations seem to die. Abraham stood in that place. His body was old. Sarah's womb was barren. Time itself testified against the promise. By all natural standards, hope had expired for Abraham and his wife.

Yet Scripture declares something powerful, that he believed in hope. This kind of hope is not based on circumstances; it is rooted in God's Word. Natural hope says, "I believe because I see a possibility." But divine hope says, "I believe because God has spoken." Hallelujah!

Many people lose heart because they confuse these two types of hope. When circumstances shift, their hope collapses. But true biblical hope does not depend on what is happening. It depends on who God is and what God has said.

When everything around you say, "Give up," that is precisely the moment God invites you to step into a higher dimension of faith so you can see his goodness. It is not a denial of reality; it is defiance of limitation. It is choosing to trust God above evidence.

"Against hope" is not the end of your story. It is the beginning of a miracle. Godly hope is not wishful thinking. It is a confident expectation that what God has promised, He is able to perform. Abraham's hope was anchored in the character of God, not in his own ability or circumstances.

Romans 4 reveals that *Abraham did not consider his own body or the deadness of Sarah's womb as final.* This does not mean he ignored reality; rather, he refused to let reality override God's promise. And this is what we do as believers.

This teaches us something vital: faith does not grow by focusing on problems. It grows by focusing on God. It grows by hearing what God has said about a certain situation or condition.

Hope becomes powerful when it is anchored in God's promises (what He has said), God's power (what He can do), and God's faithfulness (what He has already done).

When hope is rooted in these, it becomes unshakable. The world often defines hope as uncertainty: "I hope it works out." But biblical hope is certainty, "I know God will fulfill His Word." Even when delay comes, hope remains. Even when things worsen, hope stands. Even when nothing changes, hope persists. Why? Because God does not change.

The strength of your hope is directly tied to your revelation of God. If you see Him as limited, your hope will be weak. But if you see Him as the Almighty, your hope will rise beyond every contradiction.

To believe "against hope" requires a different kind of faith - a faith that refuses to surrender to what is seen. Abraham's faith had three defining characteristics:

1.  He refused to be weakened by circumstances.

    The Bible says he "considered not" his own body. This does not mean ignorance, but it means he did not allow it to dominate his thinking. This is what God requires of us; That we will not focus on the problem but trust His word.

2.  He did not stagger at the promise. Doubt causes instability. But Abraham remained steady. He did not fluctuate between belief and unbelief.
3.  He gave glory to God. Even before the promise manifested, Abraham praised God. This is one of the highest expressions of faith, thanking God in advance.

Faith that believes against hope is not passive; it is active. It speaks, declares, and stands firm.

When you are in a situation where nothing makes sense, this is your moment to do this:

Speak God's Word over your life. Remember that God does not do anything except by His word. John 1:3

Reject discouraging thoughts. This is the time you think faith, remain positive even when things seem to be going down. Romans 12:2

Strengthen yourself through prayer and praise. When Paul and Silas were in jail, they looked beyond their current situation and opted to sing hymns and pray to God. (Acts 16). Through that act of faith, God brought them deliverance from the jailhouse. Let us make praying and praising a habit.

Faith does not wait for evidence; it is the evidence, and it creates evidence. Every miracle begins where human ability ends. If everything were possible naturally, faith would not be necessary. But God allows us to reach the end of ourselves so we can experience the fullness of Him. *"Against hope, believe in hope" is not just a one-time act; It is a lifestyle.* (Romans 4:18)

There will be seasons when doors seem closed, prayers seem unanswered, and promises seem delayed. In those moments, you must choose hope deliberately. Here's how to live this out daily:

1. Feed your hope with God's Word: Hope grows when you meditate on God's promises. Starve your doubt by focusing on the word of truth.

2. Guard your thoughts: Negative thinking weakens hope. Replace every discouraging thought with what God has said. Because the word He (God) has spoken shall surely prevail.

3. Speak life consistently: Your words either strengthen your hope or weaken it. Speak in alignment with God's promises.

4. Surround yourself with people of faith: Environment matters. Stay connected to people and messages that build your belief. This is important because a bad company corrupts good morals.

5. Refuse to quit: The greatest enemy of hope is giving up. As long as you hold on, your story is not over. *A man in the bible called Jabez had his life transformed by God after many setbacks.* 1 Chronicles 4:9-10.

Abraham eventually received what was promised. What once seemed impossible became reality. His story is proof that hope in God never ends in disappointment. Hallelujah!

The same God who fulfilled His promise to Abraham and my mother is still at work today. So, when everything says "no," when human reasoning and assumption say "impossible," and when time says "too late", remember this: You are called to believe, not because you see hope… but because you know the God of hope can make things good. Against hope, believe in hope.

Think of Job. He lost everything - wealth, children, health, and still said, *"Though He slay me, yet will I trust Him."* (Job 13:15)

Job didn't understand why he suffered, but he never let go of who God was. In the end, God restored him - not just double in possessions, but deeper in understanding. Sometimes God's goodness is not about preventing the storm, but about preserving us through it. God can allow it if He knows it will ultimately work for your good. He never promised a life without trouble, but He did promise His presence, His peace, and His purpose in the midst of it all.

**Responding to God's Goodness**

When we truly see how good God is, it demands a response. Gratitude becomes our language. Worship becomes our lifestyle, and joy becomes our mood. We stop asking, "Why me?" and start saying, "Thank You, Lord."

Romans 2:4 says, *"Do you not realize that God's goodness is intended to lead you to repentance?"*

His goodness draws us closer, not because of fear but because of love. We don't serve God to earn His goodness - we serve Him because of His goodness.

Every act of obedience, every song of praise, every step of faith becomes a "thank You" to the God who has been endlessly good to us.

## A Good God in a Broken World

Someone asked me a question some time ago "Pastor, why will a good God allow evil in this world?" It is very concerning, and I respected her views, but I also knew that she needed more understanding about the nature of God. Understanding God's nature will help address such issues. God's nature is good.

We live in a world that's confused about good and evil. What's right is often called wrong, and what's wrong is often celebrated.

But in the midst of moral confusion, God remains the standard of goodness.

Psalm 119:68 says, *"You are good, and what You do is good."*

That's the foundation of our faith: God is good, and what He does is good. Even when we don't understand, we can trust that His motives are pure and His heart is kind.

The world's definition of "good" changes with opinion, culture, and time, but God's definition is eternal. His goodness doesn't depend on human approval; it stands firm like a mountain that cannot be moved.

## Living in the Light of His Character

To know God's character is to walk in peace. You can face uncertainty with confidence, because you know the One who holds tomorrow. You can forgive others more freely because you know how good God has been to you. You can wait patiently, because you trust that His timing flows from His perfect heart.

When you know God's character, your heart becomes anchored in hope. You stop living by feelings and start living by faith.

## You Can Trust God

God is not like a man, and God is not like a woman. We have flaws as humans, but not the perfect God. He doesn't deceive, manipulate, or disappoint. God does not break promises or change His mind. He doesn't play favorites or hold grudges. He is faithful, He is merciful, He is holy, He is good.

If you could peel back every layer of mystery and see the heart of God as it truly is, you would find nothing but goodness, love, and compassion.

# Chapter 3: Created in the Goodness of God

We were formed out of Goodness. If you've ever doubted your worth, go back to the beginning. Before sin, before shame, before failure, there was goodness.

Genesis 1:26-27 says:

*"Then God said, 'Let us make mankind in our image, in our likeness…So God created mankind in His own image, in the image of God He created them; male and female He created them."*

Every word in that passage reveals intention, purpose, and love. You were not an accident of biology or a random coincidence of creation. You were handcrafted in the image of a good God. Ephesians 2:10 says, "For we are His workmanship, created in Christ Jesus for good works, which God prepared beforehand that we should walk in them." And because God is good, what He makes is good." You were born out of goodness, designed to reflect God's character and carry His presence and serve His purpose.

## God Saw That It Was Very Good

At the end of creation week, after forming everything, light, land, animals, sea, and sky, God made humanity. Then He looked at all He had created and declared,

*"It is very good."* (Genesis 1:31). Note, not just "good," but very good.

In Hebrew, the phrase *"tov meod"* (very good) means exceedingly beautiful, excellent, and pleasing in every way.

When God looked at you, humanity, the crown of His creation, He smiled.

Imagine that: before you ever took a breath, before you ever made a mistake, before you ever proved anything, God looked at you and said, "This is good."

His goodness was expressed in your design. You were made to reflect His creativity, His intelligence, His love, and His moral goodness.

**The Image of a Good God**

To be made in God's image means we carry a piece of His nature within us. We have the capacity to love, to create, to forgive, to lead, and to worship. We have the ability to choose what is right and to reflect His goodness in the world.

Psalm 8:4-5 says,

*"What is man that You are mindful of him, and the son of man that You visit him? For You have made him a*

*little lower than the angels, and crowned him with glory and honor."*

From the very beginning, God placed His glory upon humanity. You were not created to live in guilt or fear, but you were created to live in goodness and reflect it on others.

**Goodness and Free Will**

One of the greatest expressions of God's goodness is that He gave us choice. He didn't create robots programmed to obey; He created children capable of love. And true love always requires freedom. That's why God placed the tree of the knowledge of good and evil in the Garden of Eden. It wasn't a trap; it was an opportunity. Love is not love unless it's chosen. And goodness is not genuine unless it's embraced by free will. When Adam and Eve chose to disobey, they didn't destroy God's goodness; they just distanced themselves from it. Sin didn't change God's nature; it changed our perception of it. Yet even then, God's goodness pursued them.

**The Goodness of God in Redemption**

When Adam and Eve sinned, God didn't abandon them. He didn't erase them and started over. He came walking in the garden, calling, *"Where are you?"* (Genesis 3:9)

That question was not for information - it was an invitation. It was the cry of a good God searching for His lost creation. Even in judgment, God showed mercy. He clothed their shame with garments. He promised that one day, a Savior - *the "seed of the woman" would crush the serpent's head.* (Genesis 3:15)

From that moment on, history became a story of redemption - a story of God's goodness reaching out to restore what sin had broken.

## You Were Made for Good Works

Ephesians 2:10 says: *"For we are God's workmanship, created in Christ Jesus to do good works, which God prepared in advance for us to do."*

The word workmanship in Greek is *"poiema,"* where we get the word "poem." That means you are God's poem. His creative expression of goodness to the world. A good God did not just create you; you were created for His good purposes. Your life is not random; Your talents, your story, your personality, your struggles, they are all threads in a tapestry woven by divine hands.

## Restored to the Image of His Goodness

Sin distorted God's image in us, but Jesus came to restore it.

2 Corinthians 5:17 says: *"Therefore, if anyone is in Christ, he is a new creation..."* Before there was sin, suffering, or sorrow, there was goodness. In the beginning, God spoke, and everything He made reflected His perfection. The sun shone with beauty, the seas danced with life, and the mountains stood in majesty.

And then, the Bible tells us something astonishing:

*"Then God said, 'Let us make man in our image, after our likeness.' ... So, God created man in His own image, in the image of God He created him; male and female He created them."* (Genesis 1:26-27)

For the first time in creation, God didn't just speak something into being; He formed it with His hands and breathed His own life into it. Humanity was not an accident of nature; we were a deliberate masterpiece, shaped by divine goodness. After creating the heavens, the earth, and every living creature, God called them good. But when He created man and woman, Scripture says:

*"God saw everything that He had made, and behold, it was very good."* (Genesis 1:31)

The human story begins with that declaration, 'very good.' You and I were not created in guilt, but in goodness, not in shame, but in splendor, not by accident, but by divine purpose. The fingerprints of a good God are on every human soul.

## Made in His Image

To be made in the image of God (Imago Dei) is to be a living reflection of His goodness. It means we were designed to carry His nature, represent His character, and share His heart with the world.

- God is loving, and so we were made with the capacity to love.
- God is creative, and so we were made with imagination and purpose.
- God is just, and so we were made with a sense of right and wrong.
- God is relational, and so we were made for community and connection.

Everything about our design points back to the goodness of our Creator. That's why deep down, every human being has an inner longing for goodness; *A hunger for meaning, justice, peace, and love. It's written into our spiritual DNA because we were created by a good God who placed eternity in our hearts* (Ecclesiastes 3:11).

## The Gift of Free Will

One of the clearest proofs of God's goodness is that He gave humanity free will. He didn't create robots programmed to obey; He created sons and daughters capable of choosing love. Love that is forced isn't love at all; it is control. So, God, in His goodness, gave humanity the freedom to choose Him or reject Him. That freedom is both our greatest gift and our greatest responsibility. Unfortunately, Adam and Eve used that freedom to doubt God's goodness. The serpent's temptation in Genesis 3 was not primarily about fruit; it was about trust.

*"Did God really say...?"* (Genesis 3:1). That question planted suspicion in the human heart.

For the first time, humanity wondered if God was withholding something good from them. That doubt, that seed of mistrust, led to disobedience, and disobedience brought brokenness.

**The Fall: When Goodness Was Questioned**

When Adam and Eve sinned, the image of God in humanity wasn't destroyed, but it was distorted. Darkness entered where light once shone brightly. Fear replaced confidence. Shame replaced innocence. Distance replaced intimacy. The goodness that once defined human nature was now shadowed by sin. Yet even in that moment, God's goodness didn't fail. It was revealed.

Instead of abandoning Adam and Eve, God came looking for them in the garden. *"Where are you?"* He called. (Genesis 3:9)

That question wasn't for information; God knew where they were. It was an invitation. A call back to the relationship. Even after humanity fell, God's heart was still to restore what was lost. He clothed them, protected them, and promised redemption. Even judgment was wrapped in mercy, because God is good, even when we are not.

**The Goodness of God in Redemption**

From the moment sin entered the world, God began writing a redemption story. His plan wasn't a reaction; it was a revelation of His eternal goodness.

*He promised a Savior, one who would crush the serpent's head and restore humanity to its original design* (Genesis 3:15). Every covenant, every prophet, every act of mercy in the Old Testament pointed forward to Jesus, the ultimate expression of God's goodness.

Through Christ, we see what humanity was always meant to be: In perfect fellowship with the Father, filled with compassion and truth, walking in obedience and love.

Jesus didn't just come to forgive humanity. He came to restore the image of God within us. He came to make us good again. Ephesians 2:10 declares: *"For we are God's masterpiece, created in Christ Jesus to do good works, which God prepared in advance for us to do."*

That means the goodness of God is not just something we receive, it's something we carry. We were created to reflect His goodness in the world. Matthew 5:16 says, *"Let your light so shine before men, that they may see your good works and glorify your Father in heaven."*

**Seeing the Good in Yourself**

Many believers struggle to see themselves as "good" because of past failures or flaws. But God never called His creation "barely acceptable." He called it very good. When you look in the mirror, you may see weakness or regret. But when God looks at you, He sees the reflection of His Son, redeemed, restored, and valuable.

Psalm 139:14 says,

*"I praise You because I am fearfully and wonderfully made; Your works are wonderful, I know that full well."* If God made you in His image, then to believe you are worthless is to insult His Craftsmanship and integrity. The truth is this: you are evidence of the goodness of God. Your existence alone testifies to His creativity, compassion, and care. So, see the good in you.

It is often easier to recognize our weaknesses, failures, and shortcomings than to acknowledge strengths, growth, and worth. Life experiences, mistakes, and even the opinions of others can cloud how we view ourselves. But seeing good in yourself is not arrogance; it is alignment with truth. You were not created without purpose, value, or beauty. There is something within you that is meaningful, something that reflects goodness, potential, and strength. The problem is not that the good is absent; it is that it is often overlooked.

Too many people live with a distorted mirror. Instead of seeing who they truly are, they see a version shaped by criticism, comparison, or past failure. Over time, this distorted image becomes accepted as reality. But the truth is: your mistakes are not your identity. Your weaknesses are not your whole story. There is more to you than what went wrong.

Seeing the good in yourself begins with a shift in perspective. It means choosing to look beyond imperfections and recognizing the qualities that make you who you are, your resilience, your kindness, your growth, your ability to keep going even when things are hard. You may not be perfect, but you are not empty of good.

And until you begin to see that, you will always underestimate your own life.

**Do Not Be Too Hard on Yourself.**

One of the biggest barriers to seeing the good in yourself is constant self-criticism. Many people have an inner voice that is harsh, unforgiving, and quick to point out every flaw.

This voice says: "You're not good enough, you always mess things up, you'll never change." Over time, these thoughts become deeply rooted, shaping how you see yourself and what you believe you deserve. But here's something important: not every thought you think is true.

Learning to see the good in yourself requires you to challenge these negative patterns. Instead of automatically agreeing with every critical thought, you begin to question it. Ask yourself: Is this completely true? Am I ignoring the good things about myself? Would I speak this way to someone I care about?

Often, the answer reveals how unfair we are to ourselves.

Breaking self-criticism does not mean ignoring areas where you need to grow. It means balancing honesty with grace. It means acknowledging your progress, your effort, and your strengths alongside your weaknesses.

Growth thrives in an environment of encouragement, not constant condemnation. When you begin to speak to yourself with patience and understanding, something changes. You become more confident, more motivated, and more open to growth. You don't improve by tearing yourself down. You improve by building yourself up.

## Recognizing The Good Within You

There is good within you, even if you have not fully recognized it yet. It shows up in different ways: The way you care about others, the effort you put into trying again, the strength you show in difficult moments, the kindness you extend, even when it's not returned.

These are not small things; they are evidence of goodness. So do not grow weary in doing good, because someday you will be rewarded. Sometimes we overlook these qualities because they feel ordinary. We compare ourselves to others and assume that what we have is not enough. But comparison blinds us to our own values.

Your journey is unique, and your strengths are specific to you.

Seeing the good in yourself requires intentional reflection. You have to take time to notice: What have I overcome? What positive traits do I consistently show? Where have I grown, even a little?

When you begin to answer these questions honestly, you start to see a clearer picture of yourself. You may realize that you are stronger than you thought. Kinder than you assumed. More capable than you believed. The good in you may not always be loud or obvious, but it is real. And the more you recognize it, the more it grows.

Once you begin to see the good in yourself, it changes how you live. You stop seeking constant validation from others because you understand your own worth. You stop shrinking yourself to fit into spaces that don't value you. You begin to make decisions that reflect self-respect.

Seeing the good in yourself leads to: Healthier relationships, greater confidence, stronger resilience, a deeper sense of peace, and joy within yourself.

You no longer define yourself by past mistakes or temporary failures. Instead, you see yourself as someone who is growing, learning, and becoming. This mindset also impacts how you treat others. When you recognize the good within yourself, you are more likely to see the good in others. You become more compassionate, more understanding, and more encouraging.

Living from a place of inner worth does not mean you will never struggle with doubt again. There will still be moments when insecurity tries to return. But now, you have a foundation to stand on. You can remind yourself: I am more than my mistakes, I have value, and there is good in me. And that truth becomes your anchor.

In the end, seeing the good in yourself is not about becoming someone new. It is about finally recognizing who you have been all along. You are not defined by what is missing. You are shaped by what is already within you. And there is something greater in you than you think. Because God specially designed you. You are God's workmanship, created in Christ for good works.

## Created for Relationship

The goodness of God was never meant to be experienced in isolation. When God created Adam, He said, *"It is not good for the man to be alone."* (Genesis 2:18)

Even in a perfect world, loneliness is not considered good. That means community and connection are part of God's goodness to us. He designed us to live in fellowship with Him and with one another. That is why love is at the center of the Christian life. To love God and to love people is to reflect the image of the One who created us. Every act of kindness, every word of encouragement, every selfless deed is a glimpse of divine goodness shining through human hearts.

**The Goodness of God in Our Purpose**

God didn't just create us to exist; He created us for a purpose.

Jeremiah 29:11 reminds us:

*"For I know the plans I have for you," declares the Lord, "plans to prosper you and not to harm you, plans to give you hope and a future."*

Our lives are not random. Every breath has intention behind it. When we live in alignment with God's purpose, we begin to experience the fullness of His goodness, where purpose turns pain into process and struggle into strength. Even the difficult seasons become instruments of God's goodness, shaping us into His likeness. Romans 8:29 says God is shaping us, *"to be conformed to the image of His Son."* That's the ultimate expression of divine goodness, transforming broken people into reflections of Jesus.

Many people try to become "good" by focusing on behavior alone, trying harder, doing better, fixing flaws, and avoiding mistakes. While effort has its place, true goodness does not begin with performance; it begins with purpose.

God's purpose for our lives is the foundation of our transformation. Before you ever did anything right or wrong, there was already a purpose placed inside you. You were not created randomly or without intention.

There is a design, a calling, and a divine plan attached to your life even before birth. John Wesley of the Methodist community would call it prevenient grace, that grace which existed long before we were born. The grace that existed before we were aware of it. That is God's goodness.

When we understand this, it changes how we view goodness. Goodness is no longer something we strive to manufacture; it becomes something we grow into as we align with God's purpose.

Think of it like this: a seed does not struggle to become a tree. It simply grows according to the purpose already within it. In the same way, when you begin to walk in God's purpose, goodness starts to develop naturally. This means: You don't have to force what God has already placed in you, you don't have to compare your journey to others, you don't have to prove your worth through performance. Purpose produces what effort alone cannot.

When you are disconnected from purpose, even your best efforts can feel empty. But when you are connected to purpose, even small steps become meaningful. God's purpose is not just about what you do, it is about who you are becoming. And as you walk in that purpose, goodness begins to take shape in your character, your decisions, and your life. God's purpose does more than give direction; it transforms.

When you begin to align your life with God's will, something begins to change on the inside. Your desires start to shift. Your mindset begins to renew. Your priorities become clearer. This is how purpose makes us good, not by external pressure, but by internal transformation.

You start to desire what is right, reject what is harmful, and value what truly matters. This transformation is not always instant, but it is real and ongoing. Often, people try to change outwardly without addressing inward alignment. They modify behavior but never experience true transformation. But when you align with God's purpose, change flows from the inside out. It becomes less about rules and more about relationships.

The more you connect with God, the more His nature begins to reflect in you. His goodness starts to shape your thoughts, your attitudes, and your actions. Even your struggles become part of the process. Challenges are no longer just obstacles; they become tools that refine you and strengthen your character.

**Purpose gives meaning to the process.**

Instead of asking, "Why am I going through this?" you begin to ask, "What is this shaping in me?" And through that process, goodness is formed, not as something artificial, but as something genuine. As God's purpose works within you, it eventually flows out of you. Goodness is not meant to stay hidden; it is meant to be expressed in how we live, how we treat others, and how we respond to life. When you are walking in purpose, these five things will be evident in your life:

1. You become more patient in difficult situations
2. You show kindness even when it's not deserved
3. You make choices that reflect integrity and Godly wisdom
4. You bring light into places that feel dark
5. You acknowledge the leading of the Holy Spirit

This is evidence of God's purpose at work. It's important to understand that this does not mean perfection. There will still be moments of weakness, mistakes, and growth. But your direction changes. Your life begins to move toward goodness instead of away from it. And over time, people will begin to see the difference, not because you are trying to appear good, but because something real is happening within you.

Living out God's purpose also impacts others. Your life becomes a source of encouragement, inspiration, and influence. The goodness being developed in you begins to affect the world around you. This is how purpose multiplies.

God does not just make you good for your own benefit; He works through you to bring goodness into the lives of others.

In the end, goodness is not something you achieve on your own. It is something that grows as you walk in alignment with God's purpose. You were created with intention. You were designed with meaning. And as you step into that purpose, you will discover that the goodness you were searching for…was being formed in you all along.

**Redeemed to Reflect His Goodness**

When you give your life to Christ, you don't just receive forgiveness; you receive a new identity. You become a vessel of His goodness, a living testimony that God still creates beauty out of brokenness. 2 Corinthians 5;17 says, "If anyone is in Christ, he is a new creation…all things have become new." Jesus said in Matthew 5:16, *"Let your light so shine before men, that they may see your good works and glorify your Father in heaven."*

The good works you do, acts of compassion, mercy, generosity, and love, are not your own goodness on display. They are God's goodness flowing through you. You were created, redeemed, and empowered to reveal His nature on earth because that nature has been planted like a seed in you.

## Living as a Reflection of Divine Goodness

Every day, you have the opportunity to reflect God's goodness in simple, ordinary ways. Practice this:

- *Speak words that heal instead of harm.* (Colossians 4:6)
- *Forgive when it's easier to stay bitter.* (Ephesians 4:32)
- *Help someone who cannot repay you.* (Luke 10:33-37)
- *Live with integrity when no one is watching.* (Job 27:4-6)
- *Worship even when you don't feel like it.* (Acts 16:23-25)

These are not small actions; they are holy echoes of our God's heart. That is being a true representation of God in the world. When the world sees your goodness, they see a glimpse of God's goodness. You were not made by accident. You were formed by a good God, for good purposes, to do good in a world that desperately needs it.

Sin tried to distort the image of God in you, but Christ has restored it. You are a living proof that God's goodness is stronger than evil, more powerful than sin, and more enduring than shame.

**Never forget:** You were created in goodness, redeemed by goodness, and destined to reflect goodness. That's who you are. That's who our Creator is. And that's why your life matters.

# Chapter 4: The Fall and the Question of God's Goodness

In the opening chapters of Genesis, the world is described with one word repeated like a melody, good; The light was good. The land was good. The sea was good. Humanity was very good. Everything God made was in perfect harmony: Creation, humanity, and the Creator in beautiful unity. But in Genesis 3, a new voice entered the story, which was a voice of doubt. *"Now the serpent was more cunning than any beast of the field which the Lord God had made. And he said to the woman, 'Did God really say...?'"* (Genesis 3:1)

Those words, "Did God really say?" - introduced humanity's first question about the goodness of God. It was a question posed to doubt the integrity and the faithfulness of God. The serpent didn't attack Eve with violence or fear, but he attacked with suspicion. He planted the idea that perhaps God was withholding something, that maybe His rules were not rooted in love but control. And that is still the enemy's oldest tactic today: to make you question the goodness of God when life doesn't make sense.

**The Power of Distrust**

The foundation of sin is not rebellion; it is distrust. Before Eve reached for the fruit, she let go of trust. She stopped believing that what God said was best, and she started believing that something better could exist outside of His will. What I have discovered is that when trust in God's goodness is broken, sin quickly follows. And sin always promises more than it can deliver, costs more than you expect to pay, and leaves you with less than you thought you would gain. The result was devastating: shame, fear, pain, and separation. Where there was once peace, there was now guilt. Where there was harmony, there was now conflict. Where there was life, there was now death. All because humanity doubted that God was good. Do not doubt the goodness of God. *(James 1:17) Every good gift and every perfect gift is from above, and comes down from the Father of lights, with whom there is no variation or shadow of turning.*

## The Fallout of the Fall

When Adam and Eve sinned, they didn't just break a rule; they broke the relationship. Sin fractured the connection between God and humanity, between humanity and itself, and even between humanity and creation. Thorns began to grow where fruit once flourished. Sweat was replaced with ease. Pain entered childbirth. Work became toil. And death, which was once unknown or a foreign concept, became a reality.

Romans 5:12 says: *"Therefore, just as sin entered the world through one man, and death through sin, and in this way, death came to all people, because all sinned."*

The fall of man introduced a fallen world, one marked by disease, injustice, violence, and sorrow. But even then, God's goodness did not vanish. It simply took on a new form: redemptive goodness.

**The God Who Comes Looking**

The moment humanity sinned, God could have walked away. But instead, He came looking. *"Then the Lord God called to the man, 'Where are you?'"* (Genesis 3:9). Those are the words of a Father, not a judge. He didn't thunder with condemnation; He searched with compassion.

He already knew where they were physically, but He wanted them to recognize where they were spiritually. Even in the first act of rebellion, God's goodness was evident: He called them, not cursed them; He clothed them, not shamed them; He promised redemption, not destruction.

In Genesis 3:15, God declared that one day the seed of the woman would crush the serpent's head, the first prophetic whisper of Jesus Christ. The fall was humanity's darkest hour, but it was also the dawn of God's greatest plan.

## Why Does a Good God Allow Suffering?

Every generation asks this question in some form: "If God is good, why does He allow evil?" It's not just a philosophical question; it's a personal one. When you lose a loved one, when tragedy strikes, when injustice prevails, it's natural to wrestle with this tension. But to understand the answer, we must first understand freedom. We must understand that God is not the author of confusion or evil. God is light, and in Him there is no darkness at all.

## Love Requires Choice

If God removed all evil from the world, He would also remove free will, because every sin, every act of cruelty, every injustice began with a human decision to reject God's ways. God's goodness is not proven by controlling us; it's proven by giving us the freedom to love Him willingly. Free will was not given to perpetuate evil but to do good. And though evil exists for a time, God's goodness ensures it will not reign forever.

*"For the LORD is good; His mercy is everlasting, And His truth endures to all generations."* (Psalm 100:5)

## The Goodness of God in a Broken World

Even in a world scarred by sin, God's goodness continues to shine through: In every sunrise that brings new mercy, in every act of kindness that restores hope, in every prayer answered in ways we didn't expect, in every sinner forgiven, every wound healed, every life redeemed. Romans 5:20 says, *"Where sin increased, grace increased all the more."* That means no matter how deep the darkness of sin runs, the light of God's goodness runs deeper.

The fall may have introduced pain, but grace introduced purpose.

What was lost in Eden has been restored in Christ. Hallelujah!

**God's Goodness in Consequences**

It's easy to confuse consequences with cruelty. When God sent Adam and Eve out of the garden, it wasn't punishment for punishment's sake - it was protection. If they had eaten from the tree of life while in a fallen state, they would have been trapped in eternal separation from God.

So even the act of banishment was mercy - a temporary separation for the sake of future reconciliation. God's discipline is an expression of His goodness.

Hebrews 12:6 says, *"The Lord disciplines the one He loves."*

A good parent doesn't ignore danger; they correct it. God's correction is not rejection; it's redirection toward restoration.

Consequences are often viewed negatively. When something goes wrong as a result of our actions, we tend to see it only as punishment, loss, or failure. But from a deeper perspective, consequences can also be a reflection of God's goodness at work in our lives. God's goodness is not limited to blessings and breakthroughs; it is also present in correction, discipline, and accountability.

If there were no consequences, there would be no boundaries. Without boundaries, there would be chaos. Consequences serve as a form of guidance, helping us recognize when we are moving in a direction that is harmful or destructive. Just as a loving parent corrects a child, God allows consequences not to destroy us, but to redirect us. This means that even when something feels painful, it does not mean God has abandoned you. In many cases, it is evidence that He is still actively involved in your life.

Consequences reveal truth. They expose areas where change is needed. They confront patterns that might otherwise go unnoticed.

Instead of asking, "Why is this happening to me?" We can begin to ask, "What is this teaching me?" This shift in perspective transforms consequences from something to fear into something to learn from. God's goodness is not always comfortable, but it is always purposeful.

One of the greatest expressions of God's goodness is His commitment to our growth. Left to ourselves, we can easily develop habits, mindsets, and behaviors that limit our potential and lead us away from what is best for us. Consequences interrupt that path. They act as a wake-up call. When a decision leads to a difficult outcome, it forces us to pause and reflect. It creates an opportunity to evaluate our choices and consider a different direction. This is where growth begins.

Without consequences: We might repeat harmful patterns indefinitely, we might ignore important lessons, we might never recognize the need for change. But through consequences, awareness increases. God uses these moments to shape our character. He teaches us responsibility, wisdom, patience, and discernment. These qualities are not developed in comfort alone; they are often formed through challenges and corrections. It's important to understand that correction is not rejection.

When God allows consequences, He is not pushing you away, He is drawing you toward something better. His goal is not to condemn, but to refine. Think of it like refining gold. Heat is applied not to destroy the gold, but to remove impurities and reveal its true value.

In the same way, consequences can refine us. They strip away what is unnecessary and strengthen what truly matters.

What feels like a setback can actually be a setup for growth. Perhaps the most powerful aspect of God's goodness is that it does not stop at the consequence; it continues into redemption. Even when we make mistakes, even when we face the results of poor decisions, God is still able to bring something good out of it.

Consequences may shape the situation, but they do not have the final say. God has a way of restoring what was lost, rebuilding what was broken, teaching lessons that lead to a stronger future. This means that your story is not defined by your worst decision. Instead of being stuck in regret, you can move forward with wisdom. The experience becomes a foundation for better choices, deeper understanding, and stronger character. Redemption transforms consequences into testimonies.

What once brought pain can later bring insight. What once felt like failure can become a turning point. This is the beauty of God's goodness; it does not waste anything.

Every consequence carries a lesson. Every lesson carries growth. And every moment of growth moves you closer to who you are meant to be. So, when you face consequences, do not lose hope. Look deeper, because God is still working, God is still guiding, God is still good. And even in consequence, His goodness is leading you forward, not backward.

In the end, consequences are not just about what happened; they are about what can happen next. And with God, what comes next can always be better.

**The Cross: Goodness Redeeming Evil**

If the fall introduced the question, the cross gave the answer.

On Calvary, we see the ultimate proof that God's goodness triumphs over evil. Evil did its worst, betrayal, injustice, torture, death - but God turned it into the greatest act of love in human history. What the enemy meant for destruction, God used for salvation. That's why we call it Good Friday. But the reality is what is good about the death of one's child? It is because what looked like a defeat became victory, what looked like cruelty became compassion, and what looked like the end became the beginning. Praise the Lord!

Through the cross, God proved that His goodness doesn't just prevent suffering, instead, it transforms it.

Romans 8:18 says, *"For I consider that the sufferings of this present time are not worthy to be compared with the glory which shall be revealed in us."*

## The Cross as the Ultimate Expression of God's Goodness

At first glance, the cross does not look like goodness. It represents suffering, sacrifice, and death. It is a place of pain, rejection, and humiliation. Yet, within this very place, God revealed the greatest demonstration of His goodness toward humanity.

The cross shows us that God's goodness is not always seen in comfort. It is most clearly seen in sacrifice. Through Jesus Christ, God chose to step into human brokenness. He did not remain distant from pain; He entered it. The cross was not an accident or a tragedy beyond control; it was a deliberate act of love. God's goodness is revealed in this: He gave what was most precious to redeem what was most broken. Instead of leaving humanity separated, God made a way for restoration. Instead of judgment falling on us, it was carried by Christ. The cross becomes the place where justice and mercy meet. This is the heart of divine goodness: We deserved separation, but we received reconciliation, we deserved judgment, but we received mercy, we deserved loss, but we received life. That is the heart of God.

The cross proves that God's goodness is not based on our performance; it is rooted in His love. Even when humanity was at its worst, God was at His best. One of the deepest ways the cross becomes God's goodness to us is through what is often called "the great exchange." On the cross, Jesus took upon Himself what belonged to us, so that we could receive what belongs to Him.

This exchange includes:

*Our sin for His righteousness* (2 Corinthians 5:21)

*Our guilt for His forgiveness* (1 John 1:9, Isaiah 43:25)

*Our brokenness for His wholeness* (Psalm 147:3, 2 Corinthians 12:9)

*Our death for His life* (2 Corinthians 4:10-11, Galatians 2:20)

This is not just symbolic; it is transformational. The cross changes our position before God. We are no longer defined by our past, our failures, or our shortcomings. Instead, we are given a new identity. This is the goodness of God in action, not just removing what is wrong, but replacing it with what is right. The beauty of this exchange is that it is undeserved. It is not earned through effort or achieved through perfection. It is received through faith.

This reveals something powerful: God's goodness is a gift. You do not have to strive to qualify for it. You simply have to receive what has already been done.

The cross declares that your value is not based on what you have done, but on what Christ has done for you. And that truth has the power to change everything.

The cross is not only something to believe in, but also something to live from.

God's goodness, revealed through the cross, is meant to impact your daily life. Because of the cross: You can live free from condemnation, you can walk in forgiveness, you can approach God with confidence, you can experience transformation from the inside out. Glory to God!

The cross is not just about what happened in the past, but it is about what is available to us now. When you truly understand the goodness of the cross, it changes how you see yourself and how you see God. You begin to realize that:

God is not against you - He is for you

You are not rejected - you are accepted

You are not defined by failure - you are defined by grace. I mean God's grace.

This understanding produces gratitude, humility, and love. It also empowers you to extend goodness to others. When you receive forgiveness, you become more willing to forgive. When you experience grace, you become more gracious. The cross becomes a pattern for how you live, walking in love, mercy, and truth. In the end, the cross is the clearest picture of God's goodness. It tells us that no matter how deep the brokenness, God's love goes deeper.

No matter how great the failure, God's grace is greater. No matter how far we have fallen, God's goodness reaches further. The cross is not just where Jesus died, it is where God's goodness was fully revealed. And through it, that goodness is now available to us every day.

**Trusting the Goodness, We Can't Yet See**

Faith doesn't mean we understand everything God allows; it means we trust His heart when we can't see His hand.

Isaiah 55:8-9 reminds us:

*"For my thoughts are not your thoughts, neither are your ways my ways,' declares the Lord. 'As the heavens are higher than the earth, so are my ways higher than your ways and my thoughts than your thoughts."*

There will always be mysteries we can't fully explain, but mystery doesn't cancel truth. Even when life doesn't feel good, God is good. We may not understand the "why," but we can always trust the "Who." His track record is flawless. His love is unbreakable. His plans are redemptive.

**The Goodness That Pursues Redemption**

Psalm 34:18,

*The LORD is close to the brokenhearted; he rescues those whose spirits are crushed.*

Throughout Scripture, we see a God who continually moves toward broken people: He sought Adam and Eve in the garden, He called Noah to preserve life, He chose Abraham to bless the nations, He delivered Israel from bondage, He sent prophets to call His people back, And ultimately, He sent His Son to save the world.

Jesus read in the temple; Luke 4:18, *"The Spirit of the Lord is upon Me, because He hath anointed Me to preach the Gospel to the poor. He hath sent Me to heal the brokenhearted, to preach deliverance to the captives, and recovering of sight to the blind, to set at liberty them that are bruised."*

Every chapter of the Bible is a chapter of redemptive goodness. God is rewriting human failure with divine mercy. That's why David could say in Psalm 23:6: *"Surely goodness and mercy shall follow me all the days of my life."*

Even when we wander, goodness follows. Even when we fail, mercy chases us. Even when we fall, grace lifts us again.

**The Restoration of All Things**

The story doesn't end with the fall. It ends with restoration.

Revelation 21:5 declares: *"He who was seated on the throne said, 'Behold, I am making all things new.'"*

One day, every trace of sin and sorrow will be erased. The same God who created Eden will create a new heaven and new earth, a world without pain, death, or tears. And when that day comes, every question about His goodness will be answered in full. The hymn writer said, "We will understand it better by and by..."

Until then, we walk by faith, not by sight, trusting that the same God who brought beauty from ashes in the past will do it again in our lives. It must be noted that the fall was not the end of goodness. It was the backdrop against which God's goodness became visible. If there were no darkness, we wouldn't recognize light. If there were no sin, we wouldn't know grace. If there were no pain, we wouldn't experience healing.

God's goodness didn't disappear in Genesis 3; it began to shine brighter than ever. From the first promise in Eden to the final promise of eternity, His goodness has never failed, and it never will. You may live in a fallen world, but you are loved by an unfailing God.

You may see evil around you, but goodness is still on the throne. The question is not whether God is good - the question is, will you trust Him even when you can't see it?

# Chapter 5: The Good Shepherd Who Never Fails

## The Heart of a Shepherd

In a world that often feels wild and uncertain, David's words in Psalm 23 still echo with timeless comfort:

Psalm 23:1-6 says,

*The LORD is my shepherd; I shall not want.*

*[2] He makes me to lie down in green pastures; He leads me beside the still waters.*

*[3] He restores my soul; He leads me in the paths of righteousness For His name's sake.*

*[4] Yea, though I walk through the valley of the shadow of death, I will fear no evil; For You are with me; Your rod and Your staff, they comfort me.*

*[5] You prepare a table before me in the presence of my enemies; You anoint my head with oil; My cup runs over.*

*[6] Surely goodness and mercy shall follow me All the days of my life; And I will dwell in the house of the LORD Forever.*

These words are more than poetic; they're profoundly personal.

David, once a shepherd himself, knew exactly what it meant to care for sheep creatures completely dependent on their shepherd for safety, food, direction, and life itself. When he called God his Shepherd, David wasn't just describing God's care; he was describing God's goodness. A shepherd doesn't exploit his sheep; he serves them.

He doesn't abandon them in danger; he defends them. He doesn't drive them harshly; he leads them gently. That's the picture of our God: a Good Shepherd who never fails.

## The Shepherd Who Knows His Sheep

Jesus said in John 10:14-15:

*"I am the good shepherd; I know my sheep and my sheep know me - just as the Father knows me and I know the Father - and I lay down my life for the sheep."*

To be "known" by God is one of the greatest treasures of His goodness. He knows your voice, your fears, your thoughts, your weaknesses. And He still calls you His own. That is how good He is. A shepherd doesn't just care for sheep as a group; he knows them individually. He can tell when one is limping, when one is hungry, or when one has wandered away. Likewise, God's goodness is not generic - it's personal.

He knows your name. He sees your tears. He understands your struggles even when no one else does. And He never stops pursuing you.

**He Provides What We Need**

David said, "I shall not want." That's not because life was always easy for him - far from it. David wrote those words through seasons of betrayal, battle, and heartbreak. Yet he could still say, "I lack nothing." Why? Because when God is your Shepherd, you can trust His provision.

- He provides rest: "He makes me lie down in green pastures."
- He provides peace: "He leads me beside still waters."
- He provides restoration: "He restores my soul."
- He provides guidance: "He leads me in paths of righteousness for His name's sake."

God's goodness is not just about giving us what we want - it's about giving us what we need most, even when we don't realize it.

Sometimes His provision looks like open doors; other times, it looks like closed ones. Sometimes it's abundance; sometimes it's endurance. But in every situation, His care is perfect, and His timing is precise.

## The Valley Does Not Mean the Shepherd Is Gone

David continued: *"Even though I walk through the valley of the shadow of death, I will fear no evil, for You are with me."* (Psalm 23:4)

The goodness of the Shepherd doesn't mean we never walk through valleys. It means we never walk through them alone. Notice that David didn't say, "If I walk through the valley," but "when I walk through the valley." This simply means that valleys are part of life; dark places of uncertainty, loss, pain, or fear. But valleys are also transitions. You walk through them, not stay in them. The same God who led you beside still waters will lead you safely through the shadows. And in the valley, something changes. David stops talking about God ("He leads me… He restores me…") and starts talking to God ("You are with me…") because it's often in the valley that God's goodness becomes most personal.

## Your Shepherd Fights for You

In ancient times, a shepherd carried two tools - a rod and a staff. The rod was a weapon to defend the sheep from predators; the staff was a tool to guide and rescue them.

David said, "Your rod and Your staff, they comfort me."

That's the balance of God's goodness, protection, and direction.

He fights off the attacks of the enemy, and He gently corrects us when we stray. Both are acts of love. Sometimes His rod feels like correction, a closed door, a conviction, a "no" to a prayer. But every act of discipline is rooted in His goodness.

Psalm 119:68 says, *"You are good, and what You do is good."*

Even when it doesn't feel like it, His rod and His staff are working for your protection and growth.

## The Shepherd Who Does Not Abandon

The image of the Good Shepherd is one of the most powerful pictures of care, protection, and love. A shepherd is not distant from the sheep; he is present, watchful, and committed. When danger comes, he does not run away; he stands and fights.

To understand how the Good Shepherd fights for us, we must first understand His heart. A hired servant may flee when trouble appears, but a true shepherd stays because the sheep belong to him. There is ownership, a relationship, and deep responsibility. This means that when we face danger, whether physical, emotional, or spiritual, we are not left alone to defend ourselves.

The Good Shepherd does not abandon His flock in moments of vulnerability. There are times in life when it feels like we are exposed, surrounded by challenges, and unsure of how things will turn out. But even in those moments, the Shepherd is near. His presence is not always loud or visible, but it is constant.

His fight for us begins with His commitment to us.

He watches over what belongs to Him. He guards, protects, and stands between us and what seeks to harm us. This is not passive care; it is active defense.

The Shepherd's goodness is seen in this: He does not wait for danger to pass; He steps into it on our behalf. The Good Shepherd fights for us not only by confronting danger, but also by guiding us away from it.

One of the greatest ways God protects us is through direction.

Often, we expect God's protection to look like removing every obstacle. But many times, His protection comes as guidance, leading us away from paths that would bring harm.

A shepherd leads his sheep to safe pastures and still waters. He knows where danger lies, even when the sheep do not. In the same way, God sees what we cannot see. When He redirects us, closes doors, or changes our course, it is not rejection; it is protection.

Sometimes the fight happens before the battle even reaches us.

There are dangers we never encounter, problems we never face, and situations we are spared from, all because the Shepherd has gone ahead of us. Even when we walk through difficult seasons, we are not without defense. The Shepherd uses His rod and staff, symbols of protection and correction. The rod defends against predators, while the staff pulls the sheep back when they wander too far. This shows us that God fights for us in multiple ways: By shielding us from harm, by guiding our steps, and by correcting us when we drift.

Even His correction is part of His protection. What may feel uncomfortable in the moment is often evidence that He is keeping us from something greater. Not all battles are visible. Some of the greatest struggles happen internally, such as fear, doubt, anxiety, and discouragement. Others happen spiritually, in ways we may not fully understand. The Good Shepherd fights these battles as well.

There are moments when you feel overwhelmed, when your strength is low, and when your faith feels weak. In those times, it is easy to believe you are fighting alone. But the truth is, the Shepherd is actively working on your behalf…He strengthens you when you are weary, He restores you when you are broken, He defends you against what you cannot see.

Sometimes the battle is not removed immediately, but you are sustained through it. That is also part of His fight. Victory is not always about instant change. It is often about enduring with divine strength.

The Shepherd also fights by speaking truth into your life. When lies try to take root, telling you that you are alone, forgotten, or defeated, His truth counters them. He reminds you of who you are, He reminds you of His promises, He reminds you that the battle is not yours alone. Even when you cannot see the outcome, you can trust that the Shepherd is already working behind the scenes.

The greatest demonstration of the Good Shepherd fighting for us is seen in His willingness to lay down His life. A shepherd who truly loves his sheep does not just protect them from minor threats; he is willing to face the ultimate danger on their behalf. This is the depth of God's goodness. He did not merely defend us from a distance; He stepped into the battle fully. He took upon Himself what we could not overcome on our own.

This act secured a victory that goes beyond temporary protection; it provides lasting security. Because of the Shepherd's sacrifice, We are no longer alone in our battles, we have access to strength beyond ourselves, we can live with confidence, knowing we are covered.

Even now, the Shepherd continues to watch over us. His fight did not end; it continues in how He leads, protects, and sustains us daily. Our role is not to fight alone, but to trust the One who fights for us. This requires surrender. Sheep do not protect themselves; they rely on the shepherd. In the same way, we are called to trust God's leadership, follow His voice, and rest in His care. When we do, we begin to experience peace that does not depend on circumstances. We realize that no matter what comes against us, we are not defenseless.

The Good Shepherd stands with us. He goes before us. He fights for us. And because of Him, we are never alone in battle. In the end, the story is not about how strong the sheep are, but it is about how faithful the Shepherd is. And His faithfulness never fails. Lamentations 3:22-23 says,

*Through the LORD's mercies we are not consumed, because His compassions fail not. [23] They are new every morning; Great is Your faithfulness.*

## The Table in the Midst of Trouble

*"You prepare a table before me in the presence of my enemies."*

(Psalm 23:5)

Note that God doesn't always remove your enemies. Sometimes He blesses you in front of them. He displays

His goodness not by taking you out of trouble, but by giving you peace and provision in the middle of it. This is a picture of victory, not in isolation, but in revelation. Your enemies will see the evidence of God's favor on your life. When others expect your defeat, God lays out a feast.

When the enemy surrounds you with fear, God surrounds you with favor.

David continues, "You anoint my head with oil; my cup overflows." In biblical times, shepherds would anoint their sheep's heads with oil to protect them from insects and heal wounds. That oil represents the Holy Spirit, the active presence of God in your life that heals, refreshes, and empowers you. To be anointed means to be set apart for a divine purpose and protected by divine power. And the result of that anointing is overflow, not just enough for you, but enough to bless others. When you live close to the Shepherd, you become a channel of His goodness. Your peace encourages in the midst of anxiety, your faith strengthens in times of weary, and your joy becomes contagious. The cup of a good life is one that continually overflows with the goodness of God.

**Goodness and Mercy: The Companions of Life**

David concludes his psalm with a promise:

"Surely goodness and mercy shall follow me all the days of my life." God's goodness and mercy are not occasional visitors; They are constant companions. Everywhere you go, they follow. When you fall, mercy lifts you. When you succeed, goodness sustains you. When you wander, grace guides you home.

This doesn't mean life will be perfect; it means you'll never face it without God's kindness close behind. Goodness supplies what you need; mercy forgives when you fail. Together, they ensure that your story always ends with hope. God's goodness and mercy are not occasional actions. They are essential to who He is. They are not moods that change or responses that depend on circumstances. They are constant, unchanging, and deeply rooted in His nature. Goodness speaks of God's generosity, kindness, and desire to bless. Mercy speaks of His compassion, forgiveness, and willingness to withhold what we deserve. Together, they form a powerful picture: God gives what we do not deserve (goodness), and He withholds what we do deserve (mercy). This means that every day we live, we are surrounded by both. The air we breathe, the strength we carry, the opportunities we receive - these are expressions of His goodness. The mistakes we survive, the judgment we escape, the second chances we receive; These are expressions of His mercy.

Many people struggle to believe this because they focus more on their failures than on God's nature. But God's goodness and mercy are not based on our perfection; they are based on His character. Even when we fall short, He remains kind. Even when we are undeserving, He remains compassionate. Understanding this truth changes how we approach God. Instead of fear and distance, we can come with confidence, knowing that we will meet goodness and mercy, not rejection and judgment.

This is the foundation of a relationship: a God who is both kind enough to bless and merciful enough to forgive. God's goodness is often seen in the everyday moments we might overlook.

It is easy to recognize goodness in breakthroughs, answered prayers, open doors, and visible blessings. But God's goodness is not limited to big events. It is present in the ordinary rhythms of life. It shows up in: Provision when you need it, strength when you feel weak, peace in the middle of uncertainty, opportunities that come at the right time.

Sometimes, God's goodness is subtle. It may not always be loud or dramatic, but it is consistent. Even delays can carry His goodness. What feels like a "no" or "not yet" can actually be protection or preparation. God sees the bigger picture, and His goodness works beyond what we can immediately understand.

**Recognizing God's goodness requires awareness.**

When you begin to look for it, you start to see it everywhere. Your perspective shifts from lack to gratitude, from frustration to appreciation. Instead of asking, "What do I not have?" you begin to ask, "What has God already given?" And as you recognize His goodness more, your faith grows. You begin to trust that the same God who has been faithful before will continue to be faithful again.

While God's goodness provides, His mercy restores. Mercy meets us in our lowest moments, when we have failed, when we feel unworthy, and when we are aware of our shortcomings. It is in these moments that mercy becomes most meaningful. Instead of turning away, God draws near. Instead of condemning, He offers compassion. Instead of ending the story, He provides another chance. This is what makes mercy so powerful. It interrupts what we deserve and replaces it with grace. Mercy says: Your mistake is not the end, your failure does not define you, there is still a way forward.

Many people struggle to receive mercy because they feel they must earn it. But mercy, by its very nature, cannot be earned. It is given freely. And God does that. This does not mean our actions do not matter. It means that God's response is not limited by our worst moments. His mercy creates space for growth, healing, and transformation.

When you understand this, you no longer live trapped in guilt or shame. You begin to live in freedom, knowing that even when you fall, mercy is there to lift you up again. God's goodness and mercy are not separate; they work together.

Goodness leads you forward. Mercy lifts you when you fall.

Goodness opens doors. Mercy restores you when you take the wrong path. Goodness provides what you need. Mercy covers where you fall short. Together, they create balance. If there were only goodness without mercy, we might receive blessings but be crushed by our failures. If there were only mercy without goodness, we might be forgiven but never fully experience the fullness of life. But God gives both. Glory to God!

This is why you can move forward with confidence. You are supported on both sides, blessed by goodness and sustained by mercy.

Even in difficult seasons, both are still at work: When life goes well, you are experiencing His goodness. When life is challenging, you are experiencing His mercy. And often, you are experiencing both at the same time.

Understanding this brings peace. You no longer have to question whether God is for you. His goodness proves His generosity, and His mercy proves His compassion. Knowing about God's goodness and mercy is one thing, and living in it is another.

To live in this reality, you must:

1. Receive it daily - Accept that God's goodness and mercy are available to you right now.
2. Remember it consistently - Reflect on how God has been faithful in the past.
3. Respond with gratitude - Let thankfulness shape your attitude and outlook.
4. Reflect it to others - Extend the same kindness and compassion you have received.

When you live with this awareness, your life changes. You become less anxious because you trust in God's goodness. You become less burdened by guilt because you rely on His mercy.

You become more compassionate because you understand both.

This transforms not only your relationship with God but also your relationships with others.

You begin to treat people with patience, kindness, and understanding - because you know what it means to receive those things yourself.

No matter where you are in life, whether you are celebrating or struggling, you can be confident of this.

God's goodness is providing for you. God's mercy is covering you. And together, they are leading you forward; Every day, every step, and every moment. You are living in the overflow of both. Praise the Lord!

**The Promise of Eternal Goodness**

*Psalm 23:6, "...And I will dwell in the house of the Lord forever."* The goodness of the Shepherd doesn't end at the grave. It follows you into eternity. Jesus, the Good Shepherd, didn't just lead us through life; He gave His life for the sheep. Symbolically, we are the sheep, and Jesus is our Shepherd.

He laid it down on the cross and took it up again in resurrection power so that we could live with Him forever. That's the ultimate expression of divine goodness: A Shepherd who not only walks beside you but died and rose again to bring you home. When this life is over, His goodness doesn't stop; it only deepens. He will welcome you to the eternal fold, where there are no more valleys, no more wolves, no more tears: only joy, peace, and the unending presence of the Good Shepherd.

**The Lord of comfort**

When you feel lost, remember, the Shepherd is looking for you.

When you feel weary, He will make you rest. When you feel afraid, His rod and staff will protect you. When you feel surrounded, He will prepare a table for you. And when your journey on earth is done, He will carry you home.

The goodness of God is not fragile; it's fierce. It's not temporary, it's eternal. And it's not conditional, it's covenantal. The African proverb says, "The one protected by the Supreme One does not fear the storm." God is your Supreme protector. So, fear not! He is the Good Shepherd who never fails, not in your past, not in your present, not in your future. You may wander, but He never will.

*"For the Lord is good; His mercy is everlasting; and His truth endures to all generations."* (Psalm 100:5)

# Chapter 6: The Goodness of God in Times of Waiting

## The Challenge of Waiting

Waiting is one of the hardest experiences of life. But it always turns out for the good of the believer. *Isaiah 40:31 says, "But those who wait on the LORD Shall renew their strength; They shall mount up with wings like eagles, They shall run and not be weary, They shall walk and not faint."*

We wait for healing, promotion, reconciliation, answers, or breakthrough.

We wait for opportunities, relationships, or even God's clear direction.

In those moments, it's easy to ask: "Is God still good?" After all, waiting can feel like emptiness. Silence can feel like absence.

Delays can feel like denial. But the truth is this: God's goodness is not measured by timing; it's measured by His faithfulness.

## God's Timing vs. Our Timing

Habakkuk 2:3 says: *"For the vision is yet for the appointed time; it hastens toward the goal and will not lie. Though it lingers, wait for it; for it will surely come, it will not delay."*

God's timeline is not our timeline. We live in moments, but He sees eternity. We see delay, but He sees preparation. We feel frustrated, but He is orchestrating perfection. Waiting is not a sign of God's absence; It is an invitation to trust His perfect timing.

Think about the Israelites wandering in the desert for forty years. They questioned, complained, and despaired. But every step of that journey was part of God's preparation for a Promised Land far better than they could imagine. Waiting is rarely wasted; It's often formative.

*Ecclesiastes 3:11says,*

*He (God) has made everything beautiful in its time. Also, He has put eternity in their hearts, except that no one can find out the work that God does from beginning to end.*

**God is good at all times:**

In the silence, God is at work. He is shaping your character. Romans 5:3-4 remind us that suffering produces endurance, endurance produces character, and character produces hope. God teaches us patience in waiting. Waiting stretches our faith muscles by strengthening our trust in God. When we can't see the outcome, we lean harder on His promises. His promises are yes and amen. Timing often matters more than speed. God's goodness often hides in the waiting, quietly molding, protecting, and positioning us for what is to come.

**Trusting When You Don't Understand**

Habakkuk also models a faith that trusts beyond understanding. He writes:

*"Though the fig tree does not blossom, nor fruit be on the vines… yet I will rejoice in the Lord, I will joy in the God of my salvation."* Habakkuk 3:17-18

Even when circumstances seem barren, God's goodness is still present. Joy does not depend on outcomes; it depends on the character of the One who holds your future.

Waiting is a test of faith, not a test of God's goodness. When we face storms in life, we should see them as part of the journey, not a trap to shame us. It's easy to rejoice when the storm passes, but the story is different when we are surrounded by the storms of life.

<u>**Learning From Those Who Waited In Bible Days:**</u>

1. **Abraham and Sarah**

They waited decades for the promise of Isaac. Yet God's timing produced a child in a way that underscored His miraculous power.

2. **Joseph in Egypt**

He was sold into slavery, falsely accused, and forgotten in prison. Joseph could have given up. But God's goodness was working behind the scenes, positioning him to save nations.

## 3. David before the Throne

He was anointed as king, yet he spent years running from Saul. God was preparing him for leadership, teaching him patience, and refining his heart.

## 4. Jesus in the Wilderness

Even the Savior spent forty days fasting, praying, and preparing for His public ministry. The wait was part of the mission.

The principle is clear: waiting is often a preparation. In our waiting, God prepares us and transforms us and uses us for His own glory.

## How to See God's Goodness While Waiting

Even when life seems paused, there are ways to recognize God's presence. You can:

• Look Backward:

Remember past moments of God's faithfulness. If He was good then, He will be good now.

Hebrews 13:8 says, *"Jesus Christ is the same yesterday, today, and forever."*

Malachi 3:6 tells us, *"For I am the LORD, I do not change; Therefore, you are not consumed, O sons of Jacob."*

• Look Around:

Sometimes God's provision is present in small blessings. Peace, friendships, and hidden doors are all evidence of His goodness. Psalm 27:13 says,

*I would have lost heart, unless I had believed That I would see the goodness of the LORD In the land of the living.*

• Look Upward:

Pray. Seek Him. Align your heart with His will, in His presence, waiting transforms into worship.

Hebrews 12:2, *"...looking unto Jesus, the author and finisher of our faith, who for the joy that was set before Him endured the cross, despising the shame, and has sat down at the right hand of the throne of God."*

• Look Forward:

Trust that every delay is strategic. Every pause is purposeful. Every waiting is leading to God's perfect plan. Proverbs 3:5-6 says, *"Trust in the LORD with all your heart, And lean not on your own understanding; [6] In all your ways acknowledge Him, And He shall direct your paths."*

Look Within:

In most instances, the good we are looking for is inside us. God specifically designed us as His valuable treasures.

2 Corinthians 4:7,

*But we have this treasure in earthen vessels, that the excellence of the power may be of God and not of us.*

*Colossians 1:27,*

*To them God willed to make known what the riches of the glory of this mystery among the Gentiles: which is Christ in you, the hope of glory. 1 John 4:4,*

*You are of God, little children, and have overcome them, because He who is in you is greater than he who is in the world.*

**Waiting is a sign of Active Faith**

Waiting is not passive. It's not just sitting idly by. It's active faith. It's praying, serving, learning, and preparing for the promise.

James 1:4 says, *"Let perseverance finish its work so that you may be mature and complete, not lacking anything."*

God's goodness is revealed when we wait faithfully, not fretfully.

While waiting, He is building perseverance, refining our hearts, and strengthening our spirit. Waiting is often misunderstood. In a world that values speed, progress, and immediate results, waiting can feel like weakness, delay, or even failure. Many see it as doing nothing, being stuck, unproductive, or left behind. But from a spiritual perspective, waiting is not passive; it is powerful.

Waiting, when rooted in faith, is an active posture of trust. It is the decision to remain steady, confident, and expectant even when there is no visible movement.

Active faith does not always look like action. Sometimes, it looks like restraint: It is choosing not to force what is not ready, it is resisting the urge to take control out of fear, it is standing firm when everything in you wants to move ahead.

Waiting becomes an act of faith when you believe that timing matters and that God's timing is perfect. Anyone can move when the path is clear. But it takes faith to stand still when the way forward is uncertain. This kind of waiting is not empty. It is filled with expectations. It says: I trust that something is happening, even if I cannot see it, I believe that delay does not mean denial, I know that what is coming is worth the wait.

Waiting is not the absence of faith; it is often the evidence of it.

One of the most important truths about waiting is this: while you are waiting, God is working. Even when nothing appears to be changing on the surface, things are being prepared behind the scenes. God works in ways we cannot always see: Sometimes aligning circumstances, opening and closing doors, preparing opportunities, and positioning people in our lives. But perhaps even more importantly, He is working in you.

Waiting seasons are often seasons of preparation. They shape your character, strengthen your patience, and deepen your trust.

Without waiting, faith would remain shallow, patience would not develop, and dependence on God would not grow. Waiting in actuality stretches us. It challenges our perspective and tests what we truly believe. It reveals whether our faith is based on immediate results or on trust in God's process.

Sometimes, what God is preparing for you requires you to become ready first. If the blessing arrived too early, it might overwhelm you. If the opportunity came before you were prepared, it might not be sustained. So, the waiting is not wasted; it is necessary.

God is not just preparing things for you; He is preparing you for things. Waiting is not always easy. In fact, it can be one of the most challenging aspects of faith.

During waiting seasons, questions arise: Why is this taking so long? Did I miss something? Is anything really happening?

Doubt, frustration, and impatience often try to take hold. This is where active faith becomes essential.

Active faith in waiting looks like: Continuing to believe even when you feel discouraged, holding on to the truth instead of giving in to doubt, maintaining hope when there is no visible progress.

It is easy to trust when things are moving. It is harder to trust when everything feels still. But stillness does not mean inactivity.

Just because you do not see movement does not mean there is no progress. Growth often happens beneath the surface, quietly, gradually, and unseen. Like a seed planted in the ground, there is a process taking place long before anything becomes visible. If you dig it up too soon, you disrupt the growth.

In the same way, impatience can interfere with what God is doing. Trying to rush the process can lead to unnecessary mistakes and missed timing. Waiting requires endurance. It calls for a steady heart and a settled mind. It asks you to trust not just in the outcome, but in the One who controls the outcome.

Waiting becomes powerful when it is filled with expectation. There is a difference between waiting with doubt and waiting with faith. Doubt expects nothing. Faith expects something good. Active faith means you are not just waiting, you are anticipating. You live with a sense of confidence that what you are waiting for will come at the right time. This kind of waiting changes how you live daily. You do not become passive or disengaged. Instead, you: Stay faithful in what is in front of you, you continue to grow and develop, you remain consistent in your actions and attitude, you prepare as if what you are believing for is already on its way.

**The essence of active faith.**

1.It is not idle - *it is engaged.*

2.It is not discouraged - *it is hopeful.*

3.It is not uncertain - *it is confident.*

When the waiting season ends, you begin to see that it was not a delay, but it was a development; You become stronger, you become wiser, you become more prepared. And what you receive carries greater meaning because of the journey it took to get there.

In the end, waiting is not a sign that your faith is weak. It is a sign that your faith is alive, steady, and trusting. Because anyone can believe when things happen quickly - but it takes active faith to believe while you wait. And those who wait in faith will always discover this truth: That the timing was right, the process was necessary, and the outcome was worth it.

**The Promise of Fulfillment**

Isaiah 40:31 says: *"But they who wait for the Lord shall renew their strength; they shall mount up with wings like eagles; they shall run and not be weary; they shall walk and not faint."*

Waiting is not wasted time. It's transformation time. What seems like a delay is often God's preparation for abundance, breakthrough, and divine blessing. Even when we cannot see the end, we can rest in the promise: God will fulfill His word. His goodness does not fail, even when timing feels wrong.

God's goodness is not measured by speed, convenience, or comfort. It is measured by His faithfulness, presence, and love, even in times of waiting. Every delay is an opportunity to grow closer to Him. Every unanswered question is an invitation to trust. Every silent season is a chance to experience His sustaining grace.

When you wait, you are not abandoned; You are being prepared, protected, and positioned. And the day your long-awaited promise arrives, it will be sweeter because of the waiting. For *"The Lord is good to those who wait for Him, to the soul who seeks Him."* Lamentations 3:25

**God's Unchanging Goodness**

*"O give thanks unto the Lord; for He is good..."* Psalm 107:1

The foundation of healing is not necessarily our faith. It is not our works. It is not our worthiness. It is the goodness of God. God does not become good when He heals. He heals because He is good. Circumstances can change, emotions can change, our bodies can change. But God's nature does not change. Malachi 3:6 declares, *"I am the Lord, I change not."*

Before we understand healing, we must understand His character. Goodness is not something God does occasionally; It is who He is continually and eternally.

## Spiritual Healing: The Greatest Miracle

*"He sent His word and healed them..."* Psalm 107:20

The deepest sickness in humanity is not physical disease. It is spiritual separation from God. Sin wounds the soul. Guilt burdens the conscience. Shame imprisons identity. Jesus came first to heal the soul. The Cross is the greatest healing event in history.

### What Happened at Calvary:

At Calvary, our sin was forgiven.

At Calvary, the separation between us and God was bridged.

At Calvary, death was defeated. *Praise the Lord!*

Salvation is the restoration of a relationship. When God heals spiritually, we receive peace with God, we gain a new identity, and we are made whole from within.

Spiritual healing is the root from which all other healing flows.

**Emotional Healing: Restoring the Broken Heart**

*"The Lord is near to the brokenhearted..."* Psalm 34:18

Emotional wounds are often invisible but deeply painful. Situations such as Rejection, grief, abandonment, failure, depression, and mental disorders. They are all areas of human life that need healing. The Bible does not ignore emotional suffering: David cried, Jeremiah wept, Elijah battled despair; Even Jesus wept at the grave of Lazarus. But God's goodness meets us in our inner pain.

The woman with the issue of blood (Mark 5) suffered for twelve years: She was physically afflicted, socially isolated, and emotionally drained. But when she touched Jesus, He did more for her than heal her body; He restored her dignity.

Jesus called her "Daughter." Healing restores identity. God's goodness reaches into trauma and brings peace where turmoil once ruled.

## Physical Healing: The Compassion of Christ

*"I am the Lord who heals you."* Exodus 15:26

Throughout the Scriptures, we see divine healing: Blind eyes opened, the lame walked, lepers cleansed, and even the dead raised back to life.

Healing is not only power, but it is power driven by compassion. That's a combination of God's power and compassion. Matthew 14:14 says Jesus was *"moved with compassion"* and healed them.

God's goodness touches our bodies because the body matters to Him. However, healing can manifest in different ways:

a.Instant healing (Matthew 8:2-3)

b.Gradual healing (Mark 8:22-25)

c.Medical healing (Luke 10:34, Isaiah 38:21)

d.Ultimate healing in eternity (Rev. 21:4)

God's goodness is present in all forms. Faith can demand, but faith also trusts.

## Restoration: Beauty for Ashes

*"He restores my soul."* - Psalm 23:3

Healing stops the bleeding. Restoration rebuilds life.

Job lost everything - *and was restored double.*

Joseph was betrayed - *but restored to purpose.*

Naomi lost her family - *but gained a redeemer.*

God does not only repair - but He also renews. Restoration means;

Joy after sorrow, purpose after pain, strength after weakness, and hope after despair.

The enemy may attack, but God restores.

**When Healing Delays**

Sometimes prayers seem unanswered. Paul prayed for his thorn to be removed. Instead, God gave grace. Delay is not denial. Silence is not absence. God's goodness remains even in waiting.

In delay: Our faith matures, our character deepens, and our dependence on Him increases. Healing may be immediate, or it may unfold over time. But God's goodness never withdraws. Hallelujah!

**Living in the Confidence of God's Goodness**

Psalm 23:6 declares:

*"Surely goodness and mercy shall follow me all the days of my life."*

Goodness is not occasional; it is pursuing you instead. When you understand God's goodness, Fear loses its grip, hope rises again, and trust becomes natural. You begin to expect restoration.

**A Call to Wholeness**

God desires wholeness in:

1. Spirit (our connection with the Spirit God)

2. Soul (our connection with self, reasoning, our will)

3. Body (our connection and contact with the physical world)

*3 John 2 says:*

*"I wish above all things that you may prosper and be in health, even as your soul prospers."*

Wholeness begins in the soul and flows outward. God's goodness is not partial. It is complete. The goodness of God: What does it do for us? It heals our soul, it restores our heart, it touches our body, it rebuilds our destiny.

His goodness is not temporary. It is eternal, and it is for you.

# Chapter 7: The Goodness of God in Suffering

## Understanding God's Goodness Beyond Circumstances

The goodness of God is one of the most comforting truths in scripture, yet it is often the most questioned in seasons of suffering. When life is filled with pain, loss, confusion, or delay, it can feel as though God's goodness has somehow been withdrawn. But the truth is this: God's goodness is not dependent on our circumstances; It is rooted in His unchanging nature.

Psalm 34:8 declares, *"O taste and see that the Lord is good: blessed is the man that trust in Him."* Notice that the invitation is not based on favorable conditions, but on trust. God remains good even when life is not.

Suffering does not mean God is absent. In fact, Scripture consistently reveals that God draws especially near in times of trouble. Psalm 34:19 says, *"Many are the afflictions of the righteous: but the Lord delivers him out of them all."* This verse does not deny the reality of suffering - it acknowledges it. Yet it anchors us in the assurance of God's ongoing deliverance.

We often define goodness as comfort, ease, or success. But God defines goodness differently. His goodness includes His purposes, His presence, and His promise to work all things together for good (Romans 8:28). Even when we cannot see it, God is actively working behind the scenes.

Suffering, then, is not evidence of God's neglect; it can be a platform for His deeper work. It strips away false securities, refines our faith, and draws us into a more intimate relationship with Him.

**The Purpose of Suffering in the Hands of a Good God**

If God is good, why does He allow suffering? This question has been asked for generations. While not every reason is revealed, Scripture shows us that suffering is never wasted in the hands of God. James 1:2-3 says, *"My brethren, count it all joy when ye fall into divers temptations; knowing this, that the trying of your faith worketh patience."* This is not a call to enjoy pain, but to recognize its purpose. Trials produce something valuable, spiritual endurance.

God uses suffering as a refining fire. Just as gold is purified through intense heat, our faith is strengthened through trials.

1 Peter 1:7 *describes this process, showing that tested faith becomes more precious and brings glory to God.*

In suffering, God also reveals Himself in ways we might never experience otherwise. Many believers can testify that they encountered God most deeply in their darkest seasons. Pain has a way of removing distractions and focusing our hearts on Him.

Furthermore, suffering develops Christlike character. Romans 5:3-4 teaches that *tribulation produces perseverance; perseverance produces character; and character produces hope.* This is the divine progression of growth.

It is important to remember that God may not always remove the suffering immediately, but He will always sustain you through it. *His grace is sufficient (2 Corinthians 12:9), and His strength is made perfect in weakness.*

**Experiencing God's Goodness in the Midst of Pain**

Experiencing God's goodness during suffering requires intentional faith. It is not about denying pain, but about recognizing God's presence within it.

One of the greatest assurances we have is that God understands suffering. Jesus Himself suffered. Isaiah 53:3 describes Him as *"a man of sorrows, and acquainted with grief."* This means that when you suffer, you are not alone; God has entered into human pain through Christ.

Hebrews 13:5 reminds us of His promise: *"I will never leave thee, nor forsake thee."* Even when emotions say otherwise, His presence remains constant.

To experience God's goodness in suffering we must:

- **Stay anchored in His Word** – His promises provide stability when everything else feels uncertain.

- **Maintain a posture of prayer** – Honest, raw communication with God invites His comfort.

- **Choose gratitude** – Even in hardship, there is evidence of God's grace.

- **Trust His timing** – Deliverance may not come when expected, but it will come according to His perfect will.

Perhaps the greatest expression of God's goodness in suffering is this: suffering is never the end of the story. God is a Redeemer. What feels like a setback can become a setup for testimony, growth, and future glory.

2 Corinthians 4:17 reminds us, *"For our light affliction, which is but for a moment, worketh for us a far more exceeding and eternal weight of glory."*

One day, every tear will be wiped away. Until then, we walk by faith, holding firmly to the truth that God is good - always, completely, and eternally.

# Chapter 8: The Goodness of God in Daily Provision

**Recognizing God as Our Source**

The goodness of God is not only seen in extraordinary miracles, but in the quiet, consistent provision of everyday life. From the air we breathe to the food on our table, God's hand is continually sustaining us, even when we are not aware of it.

Matthew 6:11 teaches us to pray, *"Give us this day our daily bread."* This simple request reveals a profound truth: God desires to be involved in our daily needs. He is not distant or unconcerned; He is a present Provider.

Too often, we look for dramatic displays of God's goodness while overlooking the steady flow of His provision. Every meal, every opportunity, every moment of strength is evidence of His care. Lamentations 3:22-23 reminds us, *"It is of the Lord's mercies that we are not consumed… they are new every morning."* Each new day carries fresh expressions of God's goodness.

Recognizing God as our source shifts our perspective. Instead of relying solely on our own efforts, we begin to see that everything we have ultimately comes from Him. James 1:17 declares, *"Every good gift and every perfect gift is from above."*

When we truly understand this, gratitude becomes our natural response. We no longer take daily provision for granted; we see it as a gift of divine kindness.

**Trusting God for Daily Needs**

God's provision is often daily, not all at once. This requires trust. In a world that values security and long-term guarantees, God invites us into a relationship of ongoing dependence.

In Exodus 16, God provided manna for the Israelites in the wilderness. They could only gather enough for each day; any attempt to store it for later resulted in spoilage. This was not a limitation, but a lesson: God wanted them to trust Him daily.

This same principle applies to our lives. God may not always give us everything we want in advance, but He faithfully provides what we need when we need it.

Philippians 4:19 assures us, *"But my God shall supply all your need according to his riches in glory by Christ Jesus."* Notice the promise is for needs, not necessarily wants. God's provision is perfect, wise, and timely.

Trusting in God's daily provision also frees us from anxiety. Jesus said in Matthew 6:34, *"Take therefore no thought for the morrow… Sufficient unto the day is the evil thereof."* Worrying about tomorrow can distract us from recognizing God's faithfulness today.

When we trust God, we rest in the assurance that He sees, He knows, and He cares.

## Living in Gratitude and Contentment

Experiencing the goodness of God in daily provision leads to a life marked by gratitude and contentment. When we understand that God is faithfully meeting our needs, our hearts shift from striving to resting.

Contentment is not about having everything we desire; it is about recognizing that what God has provided is enough for this moment. 1 Timothy 6:8 says, *"And having food and raiment let us be therewith content."*

Gratitude transforms how we see our lives. Instead of focusing on what we lack, we begin to appreciate what we have. This does not mean we ignore challenges or desires, but it means we anchor our hearts in God's faithfulness.

God's provision is not always material. Sometimes He provides strength in weakness, peace in uncertainty, or wisdom in confusion. These are just as vital as physical needs.

Jesus demonstrated this truth when He fed the multitudes with limited resources. What seemed insufficient became more than enough in His hands. This reminds us that God's provision is not limited by what we see; He can multiply what we have.

As we walk daily with God, we learn to trust His provision, give thanks in all things, and rest in His goodness.

# Chapter 9: The Goodness of God Through Jesus Christ

## The Ultimate Expression of God's Goodness

The goodness of God is most clearly and powerfully revealed through Jesus Christ. While creation shows His power and provision displays His care, it is through Jesus that we fully see the heart of God toward humanity.

John 3:16 declares, *"For God so loved the world, that he gave his only begotten Son..."* This is the ultimate expression of divine goodness, God giving Himself for us. His goodness is not distant or abstract; it is personal, sacrificial, and intentional.

Humanity was separated from God because of sin, unable to bridge the gap on its own. Yet, in His goodness, God made a way. Jesus did not come merely to teach or inspire - He came to save. Romans 5:8 says, *"But God commendeth his love toward us, in that, while we were yet sinners, Christ died for us."*

This means God's goodness is not based on our performance. It is rooted in His grace. Before we sought Him, He reached out to us. Before we changed, He loved us.

Jesus is the visible image of the invisible God. Through His life, we see compassion, mercy, healing, forgiveness, and truth in action. Every miracle, every teaching, and ultimately the cross, reveals a God who is deeply good and deeply committed to redeeming His people.

*Acts 10:38 says, "How God anointed Jesus of Nazareth with the Holy Spirit and with power, who went about doing good and healing all who were oppressed by the devil, for God was with Him."*

The goodness of God through Jesus Christ is one of the most tender and transformative aspects of His nature. It is not merely a gentle attribute; it is a powerful force that reaches into the depths of human brokenness and brings restoration, hope, and life. Nowhere is the kindness of God more clearly revealed than through Jesus Christ. In Him, kindness is not just described; it is demonstrated, embodied, and made accessible to all.

From the moment Jesus entered the world, God's goodness took on human form. The incarnation itself is an act of divine goodness. That the Creator of the universe would step into creation, clothe Himself in humanity, and dwell among us reveals a level of compassion that surpasses human understanding. God did not remain distant from our pain. He came near.

Jesus did not come to condemn the world, but to save it. His mission was rooted in love but expressed through kindness. Every step He took, every word He spoke, and every miracle He performed reflected the heart of a God who is good beyond measure. *John 3:17 tells us, "For God did not send His Son into the world to condemn the world, but that the world through Him might be saved"*

## God's Goodness That Meets Us Where We Are

One of the most striking aspects of Jesus' ministry is His willingness to meet people exactly where they were. He did not wait for them to become perfect or worthy. He approached the broken, the rejected, the sinful, and the outcast with compassion and grace.

He spoke with those others avoided. He touched those others feared. He welcomed those others condemned. Whether it was a tax collector, a leper, or someone caught in sin, Jesus consistently demonstrated that God's kindness is not reserved for the righteous but extended to all.

This truth is deeply comforting. It means that no matter where we are in life, no matter how far we feel from God, His kindness reaches us. It meets us in our struggles, our doubts, and even our failures.

God's goodness does not begin after we change; it is what leads us to change. The goodness of God brings repentance.

We also see that throughout His ministry, Jesus revealed God's kindness through acts of healing and restoration. The blind received sight, the lame walked, the sick were made whole, and the oppressed were set free. These miracles were not merely displays of power; they were expressions of compassion.

Every healing was a message that ***God cares.***

Jesus did not see people as problems to be fixed, but as individuals to be loved. He was moved with compassion, and His kindness brought both physical and spiritual restoration.

But His healing went beyond the physical. He restored dignity to the forgotten. He gave hope to the hopeless. He spoke peace to troubled hearts.

Even today, the kindness of God continues to heal. While the methods may vary, the heart of God remains the same. He is still restoring, still renewing, still bringing wholeness to those who come to Him.

**Goodness That Forgives Freely**

Perhaps one of the most profound expressions of God's kindness through Jesus is forgiveness. In a world where people often receive what they deserve, God offers what they do not deserve-grace.

Jesus forgave sins in ways that shocked those around Him. He did not ignore sin, but He addressed it with mercy. Instead of condemnation, He offered redemption. Instead of rejection, He extended acceptance.

Even on the cross, in the midst of suffering, Jesus demonstrated extraordinary goodness by praying for those who crucified Him. This moment captures the heart of God, kindness that persists even in the face of injustice and pain.

Forgiveness is not weakness; it is strength. It is a reflection of God's character. Through Jesus, we see that God's kindness is not conditional upon our behavior; it is rooted in His love. And this goodness invites us into a new way of living. As we receive His forgiveness, we are empowered to forgive others.

## Reconciliation

The ultimate expression of God's goodness is found in the sacrifice of Jesus Christ. The cross stands as the greatest demonstration of divine love and mercy.

Jesus did not die for a perfect people. He died for a broken world. His sacrifice was intentional, purposeful, and motivated by love. Through His death and resurrection, He made a way for humanity to be reconciled to God.

This is the depth of God's goodness: He gave what was most precious to restore what was most broken.

The cross reminds us that God's kindness is not superficial; it is sacrificial. It costs something. It required surrender. And yet, it was given freely. When we truly understand the cross, we begin to see the fullness of God's kindness. It is not just about what He gives us; it is about what He gave us.

The goodness of God is not passive; it is transformative. When people encountered Jesus, their lives were changed. Not just externally, but internally. The proud ones became humble. The fearful ones became bold. The lost found purpose. The broken were made whole. This transformation is still happening today. When we experience the goodness of God through Jesus Christ, it changes how we think, how we live, and how we relate to others.

When we begin to reflect His goodness in our own lives, we become more patient, more compassionate, more forgiving. His kindness reshapes our hearts and aligns us with His character.

This is the beauty of God's goodness; It does not leave us as we are. It renews us from the inside out.

**Goodness That Invites Relationship**

God's kindness is not just about acts; it is about a relationship. Through Jesus Christ, we are invited into a personal and intimate relationship with God. *Isaiah 1:18 says, "Come now, and let us reason together," Says the LORD, "Though your sins are like scarlet, they shall be as white as snow; Though they are red like crimson, they shall be as wool.*

This invitation is open to all. It is not based on merit, but on grace. God desires to be known, and His kindness draws us closer to Him. Jesus revealed a God who is not distant or unreachable, but near and accessible. He taught that God is a loving Father, one who cares, provides, and listens. Through Christ, we are no longer strangers; we are welcomed, accepted, and loved.

This relationship is the foundation of our faith. It is sustained not by obligation, but by love. And at the center of that love is the goodness of God.

## Living in the Light of His Goodness

Understanding the goodness of God through Jesus Christ is not just about knowledge; it is about response. When we truly grasp His goodness, it calls us to live differently.

We are called to extend the same kindness we have received. To love others as Christ has loved us. To show compassion, offer forgiveness, and serve with humility.

Goodness becomes a way of life; A reflection of the God we follow. In a world often marked by harshness and division, goodness stands out. It has the power to heal wounds, restore relationships, and point people to God.

As we walk in the goodness of God, we become living testimonies of His grace. The goodness of God through Jesus Christ is one of the greatest gifts we have ever received. It is a goodness that meets us where we are, heals our wounds, forgives our sins, and restores our lives. It is a goodness that was demonstrated through the life, death, and resurrection of Jesus; A goodness that continues to transform lives today.

As you reflect on this truth, may you not only understand God's goodness but experience it deeply. And as you experience it, may you share it freely with others.

For in Jesus Christ, we see the heart of God, and that heart is full of goodness.

**The Goodness of God Revealed in the Cross for All**

The cross stands as the central demonstration of God's goodness. At first glance, it appears to be a place of suffering and defeat. But in reality, it is the place where God's love and justice meet perfectly.

On the cross, Jesus bore the weight of sin so that we could receive forgiveness. Isaiah 53:5 says, *"He was wounded for our transgressions… and with his stripes we are healed."* What we deserved, He took upon Himself. What He deserved, He offers to us, righteousness, peace, and eternal life. This is the goodness of God: not giving us what we deserve but giving us what we could never earn.

Through Jesus' sacrifice, we are reconciled to God. Colossians 1:13-14 tells us that *we have been delivered from the power of darkness and translated into the kingdom of His dear Son.* This is not just a theological truth; it is a life-changing reality.

The cross of Jesus Christ stands at the center of the Christian faith as the most powerful and profound revelation of God's goodness. It is more than a symbol; it is the ultimate expression of divine love, mercy, justice, and grace. At first glance, the cross may appear to be a place of suffering, shame, and defeat. But in truth, it is the place where God's goodness is most clearly displayed.

To fully understand the goodness of God, one must look to the cross. It is there that God's heart is unveiled, His character is revealed, and His plan for humanity is fulfilled. The cross tells a story, a story of redemption, sacrifice, and overwhelming love.

**The Cross Reveals God's Love in Action**

God's goodness is inseparable from His love. While love can be spoken, the cross shows love in action. It is one thing to say, "I love you," but it is another to demonstrate that love through sacrifice.

The cross is the ultimate demonstration of God's love for humanity. It shows that God did not remain distant from our brokenness but chose to enter it. He gave His Son, not because we deserved it, but because He desired to restore us.

This love is not conditional. It does not depend on our performance or worthiness. The cross proves that God's goodness reaches us even in our worst condition. It is a love that pursues, redeems, and restores.

When we look at the cross, we are reminded that God's goodness is not abstract; it is personal. It is directed toward us, individually and collectively.

**The Cross Reveals God's Mercy**

Mercy is a central expression of God's goodness, and the cross is where mercy is most vividly displayed. Humanity, burdened by sin, stood in need of judgment. Justice required accountability. Yet, instead of leaving humanity to bear the full weight of sin, God extended mercy.

At the cross, Jesus took upon Himself what we deserved. The punishment that should have fallen on humanity was placed upon Him. This act of substitution is a powerful expression of God's goodness.

Mercy does not ignore sin; it addresses it with compassion. The cross shows that God takes sin seriously yet chooses to respond with grace. This truth is life-changing. It means that no matter our past, no matter our failures, God's mercy is available. The cross stands as an open invitation to receive forgiveness and be made new.

Some may struggle to reconcile the idea of a just God with a good God. But the cross reveals that these two attributes are not in conflict; they are perfectly united.

God's justice demands that sin be addressed. His goodness desires that humanity be saved. At the cross, both are fulfilled.

Jesus bore the consequences of sin, satisfying the demands of justice, while making a way for mercy to flow freely. This is the brilliance of God's plan; He did not compromise His justice to show goodness, nor did He withhold His goodness to uphold justice. He accomplished both through the sacrifice of Christ.

This reveals a deeper dimension of God's goodness. It is not shallow or sentimental; it is righteous, holy, and complete.

**The Cross Reveals the Depth of God's Sacrifice**

True goodness often involves sacrifice, and the cross represents the greatest sacrifice ever made. God gave what was most precious, His Son, for the sake of humanity.

This was not an afterthought or a reluctant act. It was intentional and rooted in love. Jesus willingly laid down His life, demonstrating obedience and compassion. The depth of this sacrifice reveals the depth of God's goodness. It shows that God is not indifferent to our condition. He is invested, involved, and willing to give everything to restore us. When we consider the cost of the cross, we begin to understand the magnitude of God's love. It is a love that gives, a goodness that sacrifices, and a grace that redeems.

**The Cross Reveals Victory Through Goodness**

While the cross was a place of suffering, it was also a place of victory. What appeared to be defeat was, in reality, triumph. Through the cross, sin was defeated. Through the resurrection, death was overcome. God's goodness did not just endure suffering; it conquered it. This victory is not only historical, but it is personal. Through the cross, we have access to new life, freedom from sin, and hope for the future.

The cross reminds us that God's goodness is stronger than evil, greater than suffering, and more powerful than death.

**The Cross Reveals God's Desire for Relationship**

At its core, the cross is also about reconciliation. It reveals God's desire to restore a relationship with humanity.

Sin created separation, but the cross made a way for that separation to be removed. Through Jesus, we are invited back into fellowship with God. This reveals a relational dimension of God's goodness. He is not content with distance, He desires closeness. He seeks connection. He invites us into a relationship marked by love, grace, and truth. The cross is the bridge that brings us back to God.

**The Cross Calls Us to Respond to God's Goodness**

The revelation of God's goodness through the cross calls for a response. It is not merely something to observe; it is something to receive and embrace. When we understand what the cross represents, it transforms how we live. It leads us to gratitude, worship, and surrender. It calls us to trust in God's goodness, even when circumstances are difficult.

It also calls us to reflect on the goodness in our own lives. As recipients of God's grace, we are invited to extend grace to others.

The cross becomes not only a symbol of what God has done, but a model for how we are to live, marked by love, sacrifice, and compassion.

The cross is the clearest and most powerful revelation of God's goodness. It shows us a God who loves deeply, forgives freely, sacrifices willingly, and restores completely.

It reminds us that God's goodness is not dependent on our circumstances; it is rooted in His character and revealed through His actions. As you reflect on the cross, may you see the fullness of God's goodness in a new and deeper way. May it strengthen your faith, deepen your trust, and inspire your life.

For at the cross, we do not just see suffering, we see salvation. We do not just see sacrifice; we see the love of God. And above all, we see the undeniable truth: God is good.

*Luke 23:39-43 says,*

*Then one of the criminals who was hanged blasphemed Him, saying, "If You are the Christ, save Yourself and us."*

*[40] But the other, answering, rebuked him, saying, "Do you not even fear God, seeing you are under the same condemnation?*

*[41] And we indeed justly, for we receive the due reward of our deeds; but this Man has done nothing wrong."*

*[42] Then he said to Jesus, "Lord, remember me when You come into Your kingdom."*

*[43] And Jesus said to him, "Assuredly, I say to you, today you will be with Me in Paradise."*

*Galatians 6:14-15,*

*But God forbid that I should boast except in the cross of our Lord Jesus Christ, by whom the world has been crucified to me, and I to the world.*

*[15] For in Christ Jesus neither circumcision nor uncircumcision avails anything, but a new creation.*

# Chapter 10: The Goodness of God in The Church Today

## The Church as a Living Expression of God's Goodness

The church is one of the clearest expressions of God's goodness on earth today. It is not merely a building or an institution. It is a living, breathing body of believers called together to reflect God's heart to the world.

In Matthew 16:18, Jesus said, *"I will build my church; and the gates of hell shall not prevail against it."* This declaration reveals both God's commitment to the church and His goodness in establishing it. The church exists because of His divine purpose.

Through the church, God demonstrates His goodness by creating a spiritual family. In a world often marked by division and isolation, the church becomes a place of belonging, unity, and love. Believers are joined together, not by background or status, but by faith in Christ.

Acts 2:42-47 gives us a picture of the early church, a community devoted to teaching, fellowship, prayer, and generosity. They shared what they had, supported one another, and experienced God's presence together. This model still reflects God's goodness today.

The church is also a place where people encounter transformation. Lives are changed, hearts are healed, and hope is restored. This is not the work of human effort alone, but the evidence of God's goodness at work among His people.

**The Goodness of God Through Fellowship and Community**

One of the greatest ways God's goodness is experienced in the church is through fellowship. Christianity was never meant to be lived in isolation. God, in His goodness, designed us to grow together.

Hebrews 10:24-25 encourages believers to gather, to *"consider one another to provoke unto love and to good works."* This highlights the role of the church in strengthening and encouraging one another.

In times of difficulty, the church becomes a source of support. When one member suffers, others come along with prayer, encouragement, and practical help. This reflects the compassion of Christ in tangible ways.

Fellowship also provides accountability. Through relationships within the church, believers are challenged to grow, to remain faithful, and to walk in truth. This is another expression of God's goodness; He does not leave us to navigate life alone.

Moreover, the joy shared in community is a testimony of God's goodness. Worshiping together, celebrating victories, and bearing burdens together all reveal the beauty of God's design for His people. Even though the church is made up of different people, God's goodness still shines through. He works through weakness, differences, and limitations to accomplish His purposes.

**The Goodness of God Through the Word and Worship**

The church is a place where God's goodness is revealed through His Word and through worship. These are central elements of the life of the church and vital for spiritual growth.

The preaching and teaching of Scripture provide guidance, correction, and encouragement. 2 Timothy 3:16 reminds us that *all Scripture is given by inspiration of God and is profitable for doctrine, reproof, correction, and instruction in righteousness.* This is a gift of God's goodness; He has not left us without direction. Through the Word, believers come to understand God's character, His promises, and His will. It is through the Word that faith is built and sustained.

Worship is another powerful expression of God's goodness. When the church gathers to worship, it creates an atmosphere where God's presence is experienced in a unique way. Psalm 22:3 says that *God inhabits the praises of His people.*

In worship, hearts are lifted, burdens are released, and perspectives are shifted. It reminds us of who God is and what He has done. Even in difficult seasons, worship allows believers to focus on God's goodness rather than their circumstances.

The combination of Word and worship creates a strong foundation for the church. It nourishes the soul, strengthens faith, and draws believers closer to God.

**The Goodness of God Through Service and Mission**

God's goodness in the church is not only experienced within its walls; it is expressed outwardly through service and mission. The church is called to be a light to the world, demonstrating God's love in action.

Jesus commanded His followers in Matthew 28:19-20 to *go and make disciples of all nations*. This mission reflects God's desire for all people to experience His goodness.

Through acts of service, the church meets practical needs, feeding the hungry, helping the poor, caring for the broken, and reaching the lost. These actions are not just humanitarian efforts; they are expressions of God's heart.

Galatians 6:9-10 encourages believers to *do good to all people, especially those of the household of faith*. This reinforces the idea that the church is a channel through which God's goodness flows to others.

Service also brings purpose to believers. When individuals use their gifts to serve others, they participate in God's work and experience the joy of being part of something greater than themselves.

Even small acts of kindness within the church and community can have a powerful impact. They reflect the character of God and point others toward Him.

*Isaiah 6:8,*

*Also, I heard the voice of the Lord, saying: "Whom shall I send, And who will go for Us?" Then I said, "Here am I! Send me."*

*Matthew 28:18-20 says,*

*And Jesus came and spoke to them, saying, "All authority has been given to Me in heaven and on earth.*

*[19] Go therefore and make disciples of all the nations, baptizing them in the name of the Father and of the Son and of the Holy Spirit,*

*[20] teaching them to observe all things that I have commanded you; and lo, I am with you always, even to the end of the age." Amen.*

**The Ongoing Presence of God's Goodness in the Church**

Despite challenges, imperfections, and cultural changes, the goodness of God continues to be evident in the church today. God has not abandoned His church; He is actively sustaining and strengthening it.

Ephesians 3:20 reminds us *that God is able to do exceedingly abundantly above all that we ask or think.* This means that His goodness in the church is not limited; it is continually unfolding.

The church remains a place of hope in a troubled world. It proclaims truth in a time of confusion, offers love in a time of division, and provides light in a time of darkness.

God's goodness is also seen in His faithfulness to preserve the church across generations. From the early believers in Acts to the present day, the church has endured because of God's sustaining power.

Looking ahead, we have the assurance that the church will ultimately share in Christ's victory. The story of the church is not one of defeat, but of triumph through God's goodness.

As believers, we are called not only to recognize God's goodness in the church but to actively participate in it. We are part of His plan, His body, and His witness to the world.

# Chapter 11: How to Recognize God's Goodness Every Day

**Cultivating Awareness of God's Presence.**

Recognizing God's goodness every day begins with awareness. Often, God's goodness is not absent from our lives; we are simply too distracted to notice it. Life moves quickly, responsibilities pile up, and our attention is pulled in many directions. Yet, God's goodness is constantly present, quietly woven into the fabric of our daily lives.

Psalm 46:10 says, *"Be still, and know that I am God."* Stillness creates space for awareness. When we slow down, we begin to notice the subtle ways God is working around us and within us.

God's goodness is not limited to extraordinary moments. It is found in ordinary blessings, the breath in our lungs, the strength to rise in the morning, the relationships we cherish, and the opportunities before us. These are daily reminders that God is actively sustaining us.

Practicing awareness means intentionally looking for God's hand in your day. It means asking, "Where is God's goodness showing up right now?" As you begin to ask this question consistently, your perspective will shift.

Instead of focusing on what is missing or difficult, you begin to see what is present and graciously given. Awareness transforms your experience from one of lack to one of abundance.

**Developing a Heart of Gratitude**

Gratitude is one of the most powerful ways to recognize God's goodness. When we give thanks, we acknowledge that what we have is a gift, not a guarantee.

1 Thessalonians 5:18 instructs us, *"In everything, give thanks: for this is the will of God in Christ Jesus concerning you."* Notice it does not say "for everything," but "in everything." This means that even in challenging circumstances, there are reasons to be thankful. Gratitude shifts our focus. It moves us from complaining to appreciation, from anxiety to peace. It opens our eyes to the many ways God is providing, protecting, and guiding us.

One practical way to develop gratitude is to keep a daily record of blessings. At the end of each day, take a moment to write down things you are thankful for. They do not have to be large or dramatic; often, the smallest things carry the greatest significance.

Over time, this practice trains your heart to recognize God's goodness more easily. What once went unnoticed becomes a source of joy and worship.

Gratitude also deepens your relationship with God. As you thank Him regularly, your awareness of His presence grows, and your trust in His goodness is strengthened.

**Seeing God's Goodness Through His Word**

God's Word is a vital lens through which we learn to recognize His goodness. Without it, our understanding of God can become shaped by our circumstances rather than by truth.

Psalm 119:105 says, *"Thy word is a lamp unto my feet, and a light unto my path."* The Word illuminates what we might otherwise miss. It reminds us of who God is and how He works.

When we read Scripture, we encounter countless examples of God's goodness, His faithfulness to His promises, His mercy toward His people, and His power to redeem even the most difficult situation.

# Chapter 12: Sharing God's Goodness with Others

## Understanding the Call to Share God's Goodness

God's goodness is not meant to be experienced in isolation. It is meant to be shared. From the beginning, God has always desired that His people reflect His character to the world. When we receive His goodness, it becomes a responsibility and a privilege to pass it on.

Psalm 107:2 says, *"Let the redeemed of the Lord say so, whom he hath redeemed from the hand of the enemy."* This verse reminds us that our testimony is powerful. What God has done in our lives is meant to be spoken, demonstrated, and lived out.

Sharing God's goodness begins with recognizing that we are recipients of grace. Everything we have, salvation, provision, peace, and hope, comes from Him. When we understand this, it naturally leads us to want others to experience the same goodness.

God's goodness is not limited, and it is not diminished when shared. Instead, it multiplies. As we give, encourage, and testify, we become channels through which God's goodness flows.

The world is filled with people who are searching for hope, meaning, and love. As believers, we carry the answer, not in ourselves, but in the goodness of God working through us.

The goodness of God is too big to be kept to ourselves. It is not meant to be hidden, reserved, or contained within personal experience; it is meant to be expressed, demonstrated, and shared. When we truly encounter the goodness of God, something within us compels us to make it known. Like a light that cannot be concealed or a fire that cannot be quenched, the goodness of God naturally flows outward from a transformed life.

Sharing God's goodness is not limited to preaching from a pulpit or standing before crowds. It is a daily calling, lived out in ordinary moments, through simple acts, words, and attitudes that reflect His character. Every believer has been entrusted with the privilege and responsibility of revealing God's goodness to the world.

The most powerful way to share God's goodness is to live it. Before people hear what you say, they observe how you live. Your character, your responses, your attitudes, and your actions all communicate something about the God you serve.

In a world often marked by selfishness, anger, and division, a life that reflects kindness, patience, humility, and love stands out. When you choose forgiveness over offense, generosity over selfishness, and peace over conflict, you are displaying the goodness of God in a way that words alone cannot explain.

People may question theology, but they cannot deny authenticity. When they see consistency between your faith and your life, it becomes a testimony that points them to God. Your life becomes living evidence that God is good.

This does not mean perfection; it means sincerity. Even in your imperfections, when you demonstrate humility, repentance, and dependence on God, you are still revealing His goodness.

## Boldly Proclaim His Goodness

While actions are powerful, words are also essential. There is something transformative about declaring what God has done. Sharing your testimony, your personal experiences of God's faithfulness, provision, healing, and grace, can ignite faith in others.

You do not need a dramatic story to share God's goodness. Sometimes the most impactful testimonies are found in the everyday moments: how God gave you peace in anxiety, strength in weakness, or guidance in confusion. These stories are relatable and remind others that God is actively involved in their lives as well. When you speak of God's goodness, you are planting seeds. Some may receive it immediately, while others may need time. But every word spoken in faith has the power to take root and produce fruit.

Do not underestimate the impact of a simple statement like, "God has been good to me," or "God helped me through that." These small declarations can open doors for deeper conversations and spiritual awakening.

## Show God's Goodness Through Love and Service

One of the clearest expressions of God's goodness is love in action. Jesus demonstrated God's goodness not only through His teachings but through His compassion, healing the sick, feeding the hungry, and reaching out to the marginalized.

We are called to do the same. Acts of kindness, generosity, and service are powerful ways to reveal God's heart. When you meet someone's need, offer encouragement, or simply take time to listen, you are embodying the goodness of God.

You do not need great resources to serve; you need a willing heart, a kind word, a helping hand, a thoughtful gesture. These can have a profound impact. In many cases, people experience God's goodness through the love they receive from others.

Service breaks down barriers. It opens hearts and creates opportunities for people to encounter God in a tangible way. When people feel genuinely loved, they become more open to understanding the source of that love.

## Share the Gospel - The Ultimate Expression of His Goodness

Romans 1:16 says, *For I am not ashamed of the gospel of Christ, for it is the power of God to salvation for everyone who believes, for the Jew first and also for the Greek.*

At the center of God's goodness is the message of salvation through Jesus Christ. The greatest demonstration of God's goodness is not found in material blessings, but in the gift of redemption. Sharing God's goodness ultimately leads us to share the Gospel, the good news that God loves humanity, that Jesus died and rose again, and that through Him, we can have forgiveness, restoration, and eternal life.

This message is the foundation of all we share. Without it, we are only offering temporary comfort. With it, we are offering eternal hope. Sharing the Gospel does not require eloquence or perfection. It requires sincerity, clarity, and love. Speak from your heart. Share what Jesus means to you. Trust that God will use your words to touch lives.

Remember, you are not responsible for changing hearts; that is God's work. Your role is to be faithful in sharing.

**Trust God to Work Through You**

One of the biggest challenges in sharing God's goodness is fear, fear of rejection, inadequacy, or saying the wrong thing. But God does not call us to rely on our own strength; He calls us to trust Him. When you step out in faith, even in small ways, God works through you. The Holy Spirit guides your words, softens hearts, and orchestrates moments that you could never plan on your own.

You may not always see immediate results, but that does not mean your efforts are in vain. Every act of obedience, every word spoken in faith, and every expression of love contribute to God's work in someone's life.

Trust that God is using you, even when you feel uncertain.

**Let Your Gratitude to God Fire Up Your Witness**

Gratitude is a powerful motivator. When you continually reflect on God's goodness in your own life, it naturally overflows into how you interact with others.

A grateful heart is a joyful heart, and joy is contagious. When people see your appreciation for what God has done, it sparks curiosity and opens doors for conversation.

Make it a habit to remember and recount God's goodness. The more aware you are of His work in your life, the more naturally you will share it with others.

**Be Patient and Consistent**

Sharing God's goodness is not a one-time event; it is a lifelong journey. Some people may respond quickly, while others may take years. Your role is not to rush the process, but to remain faithful.

Consistency builds trust. Over time, people will see the reality of your faith and the authenticity of your message. Even if they do not respond immediately, your life may plant seeds that will grow later. Do not grow discouraged. God is always at work, even when you cannot see it.

Sharing God's goodness is one of the greatest privileges we have as believers. It is an opportunity to participate in God's work and to impact lives for eternity. It is not reserved for a select few, but available to anyone willing to live, speak, and act in faith.

As you reflect His goodness, speak of His faithfulness, serve with love, and share the message of salvation, you become a vessel through which others can encounter God.

The world is in desperate need of hope, truth, and love. And through you, God desires to reveal His goodness to those around you. So go, live it, speak it, and share it.

Let your life be a testimony that declares that God is good.

**Sharing Through Your Testimony**

One of the most powerful ways to share God's goodness is through your personal testimony. Your story is unique, and it carries the evidence of God's work in your life.

Revelation 12:11 says, *"And they overcame him by the blood of the Lamb, and by the word of their testimony."* This shows that testimony is not just storytelling; it is spiritual power.

You do not need a dramatic or extraordinary story to share God's goodness. Even the simple ways God has helped you, guided you, or sustained you can encourage someone else.

Your testimony makes God's goodness real and relatable. It shows others that God is not distant; He is actively involved in the lives of His people. When sharing your testimony, do this:

1. Be honest about where you were

2. Highlight what God has done

3. Point others to Him, not yourself

Sometimes, the very thing you have gone through is what God will use to reach someone else. Your past struggles can become a bridge to someone's healing.

Do not underestimate the impact of your story. What seems small to you may be life-changing for someone else.

## Sharing Through Acts of Kindness and Love

God's goodness is not only spoken of but also demonstrated. Acts of kindness and love are powerful ways to share His goodness with others.

In Matthew 5:16, Jesus teaches, *"Let your light so shine before men, that they may see your good works, and glorify your Father which is in heaven."* Our actions can point people to God.

Kindness reflects the heart of God. When we show compassion, patience, and generosity, we mirror His character. These actions often speak louder than words.

Simple acts can have a profound impact: We do this by helping someone in need, offering encouragement, showing patience in difficult situations, and giving without expecting anything in return.

These moments may seem small, but they can open doors for deeper conversations about God's goodness.

Love is at the center of it all. 1 Corinthians 13 reminds us that *without love, our actions lose their meaning*. When we act from genuine love, people experience not just our kindness, but God's goodness through us. In a world where many feel unseen and uncared for, even the smallest act of love can make a significant difference.

**Sharing Through Words of Encouragement and Truth**

Words have the power to build up or tear down. When used wisely, they can be a powerful tool for sharing God's goodness.

Proverbs 16:24 says, *"Pleasant words are as a honeycomb, sweet to the soul, and health to the bones."* Encouraging words can bring healing, hope, and strength.

Speaking God's truth into someone's life can remind them of His goodness, even when they cannot see it themselves. This may include: Sharing a Scripture, offering a word of encouragement, praying with someone, or speaking hope into a difficult situation.

Sometimes, people need to hear that God has not forgotten them. Your words can be the reminder they need.

It is also important to listen. Sharing God's goodness is not just about speaking; it is about understanding others and meeting them where they are. Listening shows care, and it creates space for meaningful connection. When your words are guided by love and truth, they become a reflection of God's heart.

**Sharing Through a Life of Faith and Consistency**

One of the most impactful ways to share God's goodness is through a consistent life of faith. People are often more influenced by what they see than by what they hear.

Matthew 7:16 says, *"Ye shall know them by their fruits."* The way we live, our attitudes, choices, and responses, reveal what we truly believe. Living a life that reflects God's goodness means trusting Him in difficult times, showing integrity in your actions, walking in humility and grace, and remaining faithful even when it is not easy.

Consistency builds credibility. When others see that your faith is genuine and steady, it becomes a testimony of God's goodness in your life. This does not mean perfection. It means authenticity. Being honest about your journey, including your struggles, can make your faith more relatable and impactful. A life surrendered to God becomes a living example of His goodness at work.

**The Eternal Impact of Sharing God's Goodness**

Sharing God's goodness has both immediate and eternal impact. While we may see the effects in small, everyday moments, the full impact often goes beyond what we can imagine.

Galatians 6:9 encourages us, *"And let us not be weary in well doing: for in due season, we shall reap, if we faint not."* Even when it feels like our efforts are unnoticed, God is at work.

Every act of kindness, every word of truth, and every testimony shared can plant seeds in someone's life. Over time, those seeds can grow into faith, hope, and transformation.

Ultimately, sharing God's goodness points people to Him. It is not about gaining recognition; it is about leading others to experience His love and grace. As we faithfully share, we participate in God's greater plan. We become part of His work in drawing people to Himself. One day, we may fully see the impact of what we have done. Until then, we continue to share, trust, and serve.

God's goodness is too great to keep to ourselves. It is meant to flow outward, touching lives and changing hearts.

# Chapter 13: The Lasting Impacts of God's Goodness Through Calvary Experience

The cross stands at the center of the Christian faith as the ultimate revelation of the goodness of God. At first glance, it appears to be a symbol of suffering, injustice, and death. Yet, when understood through the lens of Scripture, the cross becomes the clearest demonstration of divine love, mercy, and redemption. Through the sacrifice of Jesus Christ, God reveals that His goodness is not dependent on human circumstances but is rooted in His eternal character and purpose.

The goodness of God is not an abstract concept; it is revealed in action. The cross is where God's character is displayed most vividly. In the giving of His Son, God shows that He is not distant or indifferent to human suffering, but deeply involved and compassionate.

John 3:16 declares:

*"For God so loved the world, that he gave his only begotten Son…"*

This verse encapsulates the heart of the cross: God's goodness is expressed through giving. He gave not out of obligation, but out of love. The cross was not a reaction to humanity's failure; it was part of God's eternal plan to restore humanity to Himself. Through the cross, we see that God is loving, who initiates redemption; God is just, which means sin is not ignored but judged; God is merciful, who made judgment fall on Christ instead of us.

The cross reveals that God's goodness includes both justice and grace, perfectly balanced.

**The Cross as the Solution to Sin**

Sin separated humanity from God, creating a barrier that no human effort can overcome. But God did not leave humanity in this broken state. Instead, He provided a solution through the cross.

Romans 5:8 says,

*"But God commended his love toward us, in that, while we were yet sinners, Christ died for us."*

This is profound: God acted on our behalf before we ever turned to Him. His goodness is proactive, not reactive. He didn't wait for us to become worthy; He made a way for us to be made worthy.

At the cross: Sin was paid for, guilt was removed, and condemnation was lifted.

The goodness of God is seen in substitution; Christ took our place. What we deserved, He bore. What He deserved, we receive. This divine exchange is one of the greatest demonstrations of God's goodness.

**The Cross as the Display of Sacrificial Love**

True goodness is often revealed through sacrifice. The cross is the ultimate act of sacrificial love. Jesus Christ willingly endured suffering, rejection, and death, not for His own benefit, but for ours.

Isaiah 53:5 says,

*"But he was wounded for our transgressions, he was bruised for our iniquities..."*

Every aspect of the cross points to love:

1. The *wounds* show the cost of redemption.

2. The *blood* represents the price paid.

3. The *death* signifies the completion of the sacrifice.

God's goodness is not shallow or convenient, but very costly. The cross proves that God is willing to go to the greatest lengths to restore His relationship with humanity.

This kind of love challenges us. It calls us to recognize that God's goodness is not measured by comfort, but by commitment. He is committed to our salvation, healing, and eternal life.

**The Cross as Victory Over Evil**

What looked like a defeat was actually a victory. The cross was not the end; it was the turning point. Through the death of Jesus Christ, God defeated the powers of sin, death, and darkness.

Colossians 2:15 says,

*"And having spoiled principalities and powers, he made a shew of them openly, triumphing over them in it."*

The goodness of God is seen in His ability to bring victory out of suffering. The cross demonstrates that: Evil does not have the final word, death is not the end, and darkness cannot overcome light.

God took the worst thing humanity could do, the crucifixion of His Son, and turned it into the greatest act of redemption. This is the essence of divine goodness: transforming tragedy into triumph.

For believers, this means that no situation is beyond God's ability to redeem. The same power that worked through the cross is still at work today.

**The Cross as the Foundation of Grace**

Grace flows from the cross. Everything we receive from God, salvation, forgiveness, peace, and eternal life, is made possible because of what happened at Calvary.

Ephesians 2:8-9 says,

*"For by grace are you saved through faith; and that not of yourselves: it is the gift of God..."*

The goodness of God is seen in that salvation is a gift, not something we earn. The cross eliminates boasting and establishes humility. It reminds us that: We are saved by grace, not works. We are accepted because of Christ, not our performance. We are loved unconditionally.

The cross invites us into a relationship with God based on grace. This is a powerful expression of His goodness; He gives freely what we could never achieve on our own.

**Living in the Light of the Cross**

Understanding the goodness of God through the cross should transform how we live. It is not just a historical event; it is a present reality that shapes our identity, our faith, and our daily walk with God. Because of the cross:

1. We can live with confidence, knowing we are forgiven.

2. We can walk in freedom, no longer bound by sin.

3. We can show love, reflecting God's goodness to others.

The cross also calls us to respond. Jesus said in Luke 9:23,

*"If any man will come after me, let him deny himself, and take up his cross daily, and follow me."*

To live in the light of the cross means embracing a life of surrender, trusting in God's goodness even in hardship, and extending grace to others as we have received it.

Ultimately, the cross is the greatest evidence that God is good, not just in blessing, but in sacrifice, not just in provision, but in redemption.

The goodness of God through the cross is the foundation of the Christian faith. It reveals His love, solves the problem of sin, demonstrates sacrificial grace, secures victory over evil, and establishes a new way of living.

When we look at the cross, we do not see defeat; we see divine goodness on full display. We see a God who loves deeply, gives freely, and saves completely.

No matter what circumstances we face, the cross stands as an unchanging testimony: God is good, and His goodness is forever proven through Jesus Christ.

# Chapter 14: The Holy Spirit and the Goodness Within Us

## The Source of Goodness Within

Goodness within a believer is not self-generated; it is divinely imparted. The Bible teaches that true goodness originates from God and is made alive in us through the Holy Spirit. Human nature, apart from God, struggles with selfishness and sin, but when the Holy Spirit dwells within a person, something supernatural begins to take place.

Galatians 5:22 says,

*"But the fruit of the Spirit is love, joy, peace, longsuffering, gentleness, goodness, faith..."*

Goodness is not merely an action; it is a fruit. This means it grows from a relationship with the Holy Spirit. Just as a tree does not strain to produce fruit but does so naturally when healthy, a believer produces goodness when connected to the Spirit.

The Holy Spirit transforms our inner nature. He plants divine desires within us, causing us to love what is right and reject what is wrong. This is the beginning of true goodness, not behavior modification, but heart transformation.

**The Indwelling Presence of the Holy Spirit**

When a person believes in Christ, the Holy Spirit comes to dwell within them. This indwelling presence is the foundation of the goodness that begins to flow from their life.

1 Corinthians 6:19 says,

*"What? know ye not that your body is the temple of the Holy Ghost which is in you…?"*

This truth is powerful: God does not just influence us from the outside; He lives within us. The Holy Spirit brings the very nature of God into the believer's life. Because of His presence, our thoughts begin to change, our desires are reshaped, and our actions reflect God's character.

The goodness within us is not something we manufacture; it is the life of God being expressed through us. The Holy Spirit works quietly but powerfully, shaping us into vessels of God's goodness.

**The Transformation of the Heart**

The Holy Spirit's work is deeply internal. He transforms the heart, which is the source of our actions. Without this transformation, any attempt at goodness is temporary and limited.

Ezekiel 36:26 says,

*"A new heart also will I give you, and a new spirit will I put within you..."*

This promise is fulfilled through the Holy Spirit. He removes the hardened heart and replaces it with one that is sensitive to God.

This transformation produces compassion instead of indifference, humility instead of pride, kindness instead of harshness.

Goodness becomes a natural expression of who we are becoming in Christ. The Holy Spirit aligns our inner life with God's will, making goodness not just something we do, but something we are.

Goodness is not meant to remain hidden; it is meant to be visible in everyday life. The Holy Spirit expresses God's goodness through our words, actions, and attitudes.

Titus 3:5 reminds us:

*"Not by works of righteousness which we have done, but according to his mercy he saved us..."*

This means our good work is not a means of earning salvation, but a result of it. The Holy Spirit empowers us to live out goodness in practical ways by:

1. Showing kindness to others

2. Forgiving those who hurt us

3. Helping those in need

4. Speaking truth with love

These acts may seem simple, but they carry divine significance. They reveal God's nature to the world. The goodness within us becomes a testimony of God's presence in our lives.

**The Holy Spirit and Conviction**

Part of the Holy Spirit's role is to guide us into righteousness by convicting us when we stray. This conviction is not condemnation. It is an expression of God's goodness working within us.

John 16:13 says,

*"Howbeit when he, the Spirit of truth, has come, he will guide you into all truth..."*

When we act contrary to God's will, the Holy Spirit gently corrects us. This is a sign that He is actively working in our lives. His conviction brings awareness of wrong, leads us to repentance, and restores us to right standing.

This process strengthens the goodness within us. It refines our character and keeps us aligned with God's purposes. Without the Holy Spirit, we would remain unaware of many things that hinder spiritual growth.

**Growing in the Goodness of God**

Goodness is not static; it grows as we yield to the Holy Spirit. Spiritual growth requires cooperation. The more we allow the Holy Spirit to lead us, the more His goodness is expressed through us.

Ephesians 5:9 says,

*"For the fruit of the Spirit is in all goodness and righteousness and truth."*

Growth in goodness involves: Spending time in God's Word, praying and seeking God's presence, and obeying the promptings of the Holy Spirit. As we grow, goodness becomes more consistent and evident. We begin to respond differently to situations. Where we once reacted with anger, we now respond with patience. Where we once acted selfishly, we now act with generosity.

This growth is a lifelong process. The Holy Spirit continues to shape us, making us more like Christ each day.

**Reflecting God's Goodness to the World**

The ultimate purpose of the goodness within us is to reflect God's character to others. The Holy Spirit does not work in us just for our benefit, but so that we can impact the world around us.

Matthew 5:16 says,

*"Let your light so shine before men, that they may see your good works, and glorify your Father which is in heaven."*

When people see genuine goodness, it points them to God. It becomes a witness more powerful than words alone.

The Holy Spirit enables us to be a light in dark places, to bring hope to the discouraged, and to demonstrate God's love in practical ways.

This is the mission of every believer: to carry the goodness of God into the world. The Holy Spirit is the source, sustainer, and expression of the goodness within us. He transforms our hearts, guides our actions, and empowers us to live lives that reflect God's nature.

Goodness is not about striving to be better; it is about yielding to the Spirit who lives within. As we walk with Him, His fruit becomes evident in our lives, and we become living testimonies of God's goodness.

In a world often marked by darkness and selfishness, the Holy Spirit enables believers to shine with divine goodness, showing that God is not only good in heaven, but His goodness is alive within His people here on earth.

# Chapter 15 : Understanding Testimonies of God's Goodness

A testimony is a witness, an account of what God has done. Throughout the Bible, testimonies reveal not only God's actions, but His character. Each story, each deliverance, each miracle points to one central truth: God is good.

Psalm 107:2 says:

*"Let the redeemed of the Lord say so, whom he hath redeemed from the hand of the enemy."*

The Bible is filled with such voices, men and women who experienced God's goodness in real and powerful ways. These testimonies serve multiple purposes: They encourage faith in others, they reveal God's nature, and they remind us of His faithfulness.

God's goodness is not theoretical. It is demonstrated in real lives, in real situations, across generations.

**Creation – The First Testimony of Goodness**

The very first testimony of God's goodness is found in creation. In the beginning, God created the heavens and the earth, and everything He made was declared good.

Genesis 1:31 says,

*"And God saw everything that he had made, and behold, it was very good…"*

Creation itself testifies that God is good. The beauty of nature reflects His creativity, the order of the universe shows His wisdom, and the provision of life reveals His care.

Even before humanity sinned, God's goodness was evident in how He prepared the earth as a place of blessing and abundance.

This reminds us that God's goodness is foundational; it is part of everything He does.

## Abraham – The Goodness of God in Promise

The life of Abraham is a powerful testimony of God's goodness through promises. God called him out of uncertainty and gave him a covenant that would bless all nations.

Genesis 12:2 says,

*"And I will make of you a great nation, and I will bless you…"*

Despite delays and challenges, God remained faithful. Abraham and his wife waited many years for a child, yet God fulfilled His promise with the birth of Isaac.

This testimony reveals: God's goodness in calling, God's goodness in waiting, and God's goodness in fulfillment.

Even when circumstances seemed impossible, God proved that His promises are trustworthy.

**Joseph – Goodness in Suffering**

Joseph's life is one of the clearest testimonies of God's goodness in the midst of hardship. Betrayed by his brothers, sold into slavery, falsely accused, and imprisoned, Joseph experienced deep suffering. Yet God's goodness was working behind the scenes.

Genesis 50:20 declares,

*"But as for you, you thought evil against me; but God meant it unto good…"*

Joseph's story teaches us that:

1. God's goodness is present even in injustice

2. God's goodness can redeem pain

3. God's goodness often works overtime

In the end, Joseph rose to a position of power and saved many lives during the famine. What seemed like a series of tragedies became a testimony of divine purpose.

**Moses – Deliverance and Provision**

The story of Moses and the Israelites is a testimony of God's goodness in deliverance. God heard the cries of His people in Egypt and acted to set them free.

Exodus 3:7-8,

*"I have surely seen the affliction of my people… and I have come down to deliver them…"*

God demonstrated His goodness through: Delivering Israel from slavery, parting the Red Sea, providing manna in the wilderness, and giving water from a rock.

Even when the people complained, God remained faithful. His goodness was not dependent on their perfection, but on His covenant. This testimony shows that God is a deliverer and provider, even in the most difficult circumstances.

**David – Personal Testimony of God's Goodness**

David's life is filled with personal testimonies of God's goodness. From shepherd boy to king, David experienced God's faithfulness in every season.

Psalm23:6,

*"Surely goodness and mercy shall follow me all the days of my life…"*

David testified to God's goodness: God protected hi and he defeated Goliath. He guided through trials and decisions. He was forgiven after his sin and failures.

Even after making serious mistakes, David experienced God's mercy. His life shows that God's goodness includes restoration and grace. David didn't just experience God's goodness; he declared it continually.

## Job – Goodness Through Testing

Job's story is a profound testimony of God's goodness in extreme suffering. He lost his wealth, his children, and his health, yet he remained faithful.

Job1:21,

*"The Lord gave, and the Lord hath taken away; blessed be the name of the Lord."*

At first, it may seem difficult to see God's goodness in Job's story. However, in the end, God restored Job's losses, God revealed His greatness, and Job's faith was strengthened.

Job 42:10 tells us that God gave him twice as much as he had before.

This testimony teaches that God's goodness is not always immediate, but it is always certain. Even in silence, God is working.

**Daniel – Goodness in Protection**

Daniel's life is a testimony of God's goodness in protection and faithfulness. Living in a foreign land, Daniel remained committed to God despite pressure and danger.

Daniel 6:22,

*"My God hath sent his angel, and hath shut the lions' mouths…"*

God demonstrated His goodness by: Protecting Daniel in the lions' den, by giving him wisdom and favor, and by honoring his faithfulness. This story shows that God's goodness does not always remove challenges, but it sustains and delivers us through them.

**Jesus Christ – The Ultimate Testimony of God's Goodness**

All testimonies in the Bible point to one ultimate expression of God's goodness: Jesus Christ. His life, ministry, death, and resurrection reveal God's goodness in its fullest form.

Acts10:38,

*"God anointed Jesus of Nazareth… who went about doing good…"*

Jesus demonstrated God's goodness by: Healing the sick, feeding the hungry, forgiving sinners, and giving His life on the cross.

The cross is the greatest testimony of all. It shows that God's goodness is sacrificial, redemptive, and eternal.

Through Jesus, we see that God's goodness is not just something He does, it is who He is.

**Our Testimony Today**

The testimonies in the Bible are not just historical accounts. They are invitations. The same God who showed His goodness to Abraham, Joseph, Moses, David, Job, Daniel, and through Jesus is still at work today.

Revelation 12:11 says:

*"And they overcame him by the blood of the Lamb, and by the word of their testimony…"*

We are called to remember God's goodness, share our experiences, and trust Him in every season.

Every believer has a testimony. Whether it is a dramatic deliverance or a quiet provision, each story reflects God's goodness.

The Bible is a collection of testimonies that consistently declare one truth: God is good. From creation to redemption, from individuals to nations, His goodness is evident.

These testimonies teach us that God is faithful in His promises.

God is present in our struggles. God brings good out of every situation. As we reflect on these stories, our faith is strengthened. We are reminded that the God who worked in the past is still working today.

**Let us not only read these testimonies but live them, so that our lives, too, become powerful witnesses of the goodness of God. Ruth – Goodness in Redemption and Provision**

The story of Ruth is a beautiful testimony of God's goodness in times of loss and uncertainty. Ruth, a Moabite widow, chose to remain with her mother-in-law Naomi, declaring her loyalty not only to Naomi but to God.

Ruth1:16,

*"Thy people shall be my people, and thy God my God."*

Ruth's journey was marked by hardship, yet God's goodness guided her steps. She found favor in the fields of Boaz, who later became her redeemer and husband.

Through Ruth's story, we see God's goodness in guiding the faithful one, God's goodness in providing at the right time, and restoring what was lost.

Ruth's life became part of the lineage of Christ, showing that God's goodness extends beyond immediate needs into eternal purposes.

## Hannah – Goodness in Answered Prayer

Hannah's story is a testimony of God's goodness in response to heartfelt prayer. She endured deep sorrow due to her inability to have children, and her pain drove her to seek God earnestly.

1Samuel1:27,

*"For this child I prayed; and the Lord hath given me my petition which I asked of him."*

God heard Hannah's cry and blessed her with a son, Samuel, whom she dedicated back to the Lord. This testimony highlights:

1. God's goodness in hearing our prayers

2. God's goodness in responding to our faith

3. God's goodness in turning our sorrow into joy

Hannah's story reminds us that no prayer is too small or too broken for God to hear.

## Elijah – Goodness in Divine Provision

Elijah's life demonstrates God's goodness in supernatural provision. During a time of drought and famine, God sustained Elijah in unexpected ways.

1Kings17:6,

*"And the ravens brought him bread and flesh in the morning, and bread and flesh in the evening..."*

Later, God provided through a widow whose oil and flour did not run out. This testimony reveals: God's goodness in meeting needs miraculously, God's goodness in using unlikely sources, and God's goodness in sustaining during a crisis.

Elijah's experience teaches us that natural circumstances do not limit God's provision.

**Esther – Goodness in Divine Purpose**

Esther's story is a testimony of God's goodness working behind the scenes. Though God's name is not directly mentioned in the book, His hand is evident throughout.

Esther4:14,

*"...and who knows whether thou art come to the kingdom for such a time as this?"*

Esther risked her life to save her people, and through her courage, God brought deliverance to the Jews.

This testimony shows: God's goodness in positioning us for purpose, God's goodness in working behind the scenes, and God's goodness in bringing deliverance through obedience.

Even when God seems silent, His goodness is actively orchestrating events for our good.

## Peter – Goodness in Restoration and Grace

Peter's life is a powerful testimony of God's goodness in restoration. Though he walked closely with Jesus Christ, Peter denied Him three times during His trial.

Luke22:61-62,

*"And the Lord turned, and looked upon Peter… And Peter went out, and wept bitterly."*

Despite this failure, Jesus restored Peter after His resurrection and entrusted him with leadership in the early church.

John 21:17 says,

*"…Feed my sheep."*

Peter's story reveals God's goodness in forgiving our failures. It also shows God's goodness in restoring his purpose in our lives, and God's goodness in using imperfect people. Do you think you are imperfect? The good news is that God does not call us because of how perfect we are. But God always works through imperfect vessels and perfects them for His glory.

This testimony is a reminder that failure is not the end. God's goodness brings restoration and new beginnings.

These additional testimonies further confirm that God's goodness is woven throughout every part of Scripture.

Whether in the quiet faithfulness of Ruth, the heartfelt prayers of Hannah, the miraculous provision for Elijah, the hidden guidance in Esther's story, or the restoration of Peter, one truth remains constant:

God is good in every season, every circumstance, and every life surrendered to Him.

His goodness provides in lack, restores after loss, answers in prayer, protects in danger, and redeems in failure. As we reflect on these testimonies, we are reminded that God's goodness is not limited to the past. It is active, present, and available today.

Let these stories strengthen your faith and inspire you to trust God more deeply, knowing that the same God who worked in these lives is still writing testimonies of His goodness today. For Jesus Christ is the same yesterday, today, and forever.

The Lord will perfect that which concerns you (Psalm 138:8).

# About the Author

Dr. Angel Abakah is a preacher, Bible teacher, author, counselor, and motivational speaker. Angel holds yearly revival conferences for young people and adults across North America and Africa, respectively. His ministry has been very transformational with tangible testimonies. His ministry is defined in the words of Jesus in Luke 4:18-19

He is a man of fervent prayer who believes in the sound teachings of God's word, as well as the dynamic ministry of the Holy Spirit. His ministry has given hope to many and awakened countless people to their call to serve the purposes of Christ.

www.ingramcontent.com/pod-product-compliance
Lightning Source LLC
Chambersburg PA
CBHW051114050726

47592CB00002B/821